TURN YOUR SALES FORCE
INTO PROFIT HEROES

For Sarah, my wife and best friend.
For Harry and Alex, our two boys –
we are so proud of you both.

TURN YOUR SALES FORCE INTO PROFIT HEROES

Secrets for unlocking your team's

inner strength

PETER BROOK

infiniteideas

First published in 2009 by
Infinite Ideas Limited
36 St Giles
Oxford, OX1 3LD
United Kingdom
www.infideas.com

A CIP catalogue record for this book is available from the British Library

ISBN 978–1–906821–02–9

Brand and product names are trademarks or registered trademarks of their respective owners.

Cover designed by Cylinder
Cartoons drawn by Steve Chadburn
Typeset by Sparks, Oxford – www.sparkspublishing.com
Printed and bound by TJ International Limited, Padstow, Cornwall

The paper used in this book is FSC certified. FSC (the Forest Stewardship Council) is an international network to promote the responsible management of the world's forests.

Mixed Sources
Product group from well-managed forests and other controlled sources
www.fsc.org Cert no. SGS-COC-2482
© 1996 Forest Stewardship Council
FSC

CONTENTS

Acknowledgements   ix
Foreword   xi

Introduction   1

Part I How to turn people into learners and heroes   9

1   *Are you responsible for the way others behave?*   11
    Understanding how our personal behaviour and skills
    will determine how others behave.

2   *Connecting the brain with building capability*   23
    Using brain-based learning to invigorate others
    in developing themselves.

3   *What's in it for the organisation?*   43
    Creating a winning team fuelled by similar ambitions.

Part II How to release the talents of the sales force   55

4   *The capabilities necessary to sell exceptional brands*   57
    Setting sales management standards.

5   *The skills to sell exceptional brands*   89
    The foundation skills for sales teams to delight customers.

6   *Packaging the skills to equip the organisation*   125
    How to construct materials to relieve corporate memory loss.

Part III My line manager is my coach and mentor **151**

7 *Inspirational sales leadership* 153
The capabilities required to coach sales teams.
8 *Lost in translation* 177
The desire, ability and confidence to train.
9 *Putting it all together* 193
Creating maximum engagement, retention,
recall and then application.
10 *Not sure/want to learn more* 203

Index 211

ACKNOWLEDGEMENTS

To realise dreams you occasionally need encouragement. The whole team at Infinite Ideas gave me the belief and conviction to write this book, especially **Katherine** and **David,** who persuaded me to embark on one of the biggest adventures I have ever undertaken. To **Richard** and **Rebecca** for guiding me through the journey and to each and every member of the team – see, I knew I would go to Oxford one day!

Prior to starting REL Sales Consulting I spent eight superb years working for Guinness and then Diageo. During these years I was so fortunate to be working with fantastic colleagues on amazing brands. The enjoyment, learning and indeed the results we achieved were directly due to outstanding leadership from every member of the management team. Leadership starts at the helm of any business. I am delighted and grateful that **Paul Walsh**, CEO of Diageo plc, agreed to compile the foreword for this book. Receiving endorsement from the leader of a significant component of your inspiration is very flattering. Thank you, Paul.

I have learnt that when you embark on new journeys in life you achieve better results faster when you surround yourself with individuals who have the skills and experience to guide you. I have always preferred praise to criticism, so the balance and effect of this, as provided by **Ken,** who has been a passionate coach to me while writing this, my first book, has been immeasurable. Thank you, Ken.

I also firmly believe in doing what I do, and I look for individuals with outstanding talent in areas where I am not so great to support me. In finding **Steve** I have had a brilliant illustrator, who has brought this book to life in a way that stimulates thinking, adds to my written words, while at the same time often making me laugh out loud. Thank you, Steve.

For the content, the people who have inspired me could fill the first two chapters. There are so many people who have changed the way that I approach working with others today. My grateful thanks are due:

- to all our clients who have worked so closely with us to enhance the capability of their teams;
- to everyone who has worked within the business, developing such fantastic solutions for those clients;
- to **David** and **Pat** for believing in me when I started REL Sales Consulting in 2005;
- to **Joost,** who has led the way for the internationalisation of the business;
- to **Tim** and **Colin** for making me realise the intensity of care you need to provide for learners; and not least
- to every person I have ever had the pleasure (or occasionally pain!) of working with. Each one of you has taught me and fashioned what I know works and what does not.

My wife **Sarah,** our sons **Harry** and **Alex** are my single biggest motivators and inspirers. Thank you for your support and tolerance over the months of writing and thank you most of all for being you.

This book has taken nine months from the first e-mail to its publication, I will leave you to reflect on the parallels that this represents!

FOREWORD

by Paul S. Walsh, CEO Diageo plc

This book, *Turn Your Sales Force into Profit Heroes*, is timely, relevant, and thought provoking.

In it, Peter Brook shows how to utilise the inner strength of the sales leadership community, using their actions and skills to develop their teams with passion, and I could not agree more with the book's central hypothesis that companies could do much more to unlock the profit opportunity in sales.

In nearly thirty years of experience working in fast moving consumer goods, marketing is nearly always seen as a key strategic lever in driving profit growth through stimulating consumer demand, while sales is variously described in some companies as unglamorous, tactical, downstream, un-strategic and easy. What a mistake.

Yes, great marketing is crucial – I would say that as someone whose career has been about building brands – but its effect is markedly diluted if the sales strategy or execution is poor. There's no point in stimulating consumer demand if the products aren't widely available, have poor visibility in store, or aren't supported or promoted by our customers – all elements which the sales team can deliver, if they are skilful of course.

For me marketing and sales are two sides of the same coin – co-dependent – and if you get the strategies and execution for both to be brilliant then your business will undoubtedly grow. One without the other won't cut it, and that's why smart companies treat sales as every bit as important a strategic priority as marketing. Our sales teams are the front line in our battle for competitive advantage.

In our business, Diageo, the world's leading premium drinks company, we have always put the consumer at the heart of our strategy. We have striven to understand our target market better than anyone else, and we have used those insights to create great campaigns. In that regard we're similar to most FMCG companies.

Where we perhaps do differ is in our strategy to treat our customers in the same way as we treat our consumers; to understand them intimately, to know their shoppers, to use those insights to improve our service to them, and in doing so to establish amazing relationships which will deliver value for both parties. We are in the business of creating an outstanding customer connection.

To achieve that goal, to hunt down that profit opportunity, we need extremely high-performing sales teams, filled with great talent, which we prize and develop. But develop in a particular way.

We believe that the traditional sales model of relentless sole focus on financial targets, will not be enough to release the full potential of the individual, and therefore will not create the performance transformation required if we are to fully leverage sales as a profit driver. Of course targets are important as a means of measuring success or otherwise, but they do not of themselves inspire exceptional performance. And that is what we are looking for from our sales teams – exceptional performance.

For us, the key to unlocking the growth opportunity in sales, to inspiring our people to create those amazing relationships with our customers, is via continuous skills development and great leadership.

We invest heavily in programmes to equip our people with the tools and training which will enable them to deliver an outstanding professional service, consistent with the standards we have set for ourselves – codified in our strategy, the Diageo Way of Selling. We value and celebrate brilliant execution.

But where we see an even bigger opportunity, the intervention where we can make a game-changing difference, is in outstanding and inspiring functional leadership. From the Chief Customer Officer – the title of the global head of our sales function – to a field sales team's line manager, strong leadership delivers the extra points of performance, the additional discretionary effort which makes the difference between good and great.

We want leaders who use our shared cultural values as sources of energy and inspiration for their teams, and this philosophy is at the core of how we select and train them. Every one of our people is entitled to a great manager.

Our overarching ambition in doing all of this work is to be every bit as good at sales as we are at marketing. Turning all of our sales force into profit heroes, and in doing so delivering competitive advantage. That is a prize worth pursuing, and encapsulates why a strategic focus on sales will always be smart business.

INTRODUCTION

To purchase any fast moving consumer product is, after all, quite simple. Take the drinks trade as an example – consumer orders, barperson pours the drink, money changes hands, till tings, mutual thank-yous and … job done. The same goes for any transaction and any product, in a major department store, supermarket or corner shop. But the companies that make the consumer products have a complicated series of hurdles to jump before that simple transaction takes place and is repeated time and time again.

First, they have to sell the product to a wholesaler, the central purchasing department of their larger customers, or individual outlet owners. Then they have to make sure that retail outlets are displaying, dispensing and promoting their products in the best possible way. There can be a lot of people in this selling chain.

Outstanding organisations create products that have broad consumer appeal. They outclass competitive offerings and deliver profitability to each entity in this complicated sales chain. To do so efficiently and effectively they rely on sales teams supported by excellent marketing, and who are highly skilled at connecting the product on sale with the needs of their customers, those wholesalers and key accounts, and their consumers – the people who buy the products.

Modern media create consumers who are more educated and sophisticated than their forebears. This leads to opportunities for manufacturers to extend the distribution of their products to many new markets. Global brands are now commonplace: they bring huge opportunities for economies of scale and commonality of marketing. Local brands, however, remain important as they maintain targeted consumer appeal. The impact of all this is that organisations need global brands supported by local priority products.

Now think about the employees of these producers. Nowadays, a greater proportion of them are ambitious; they are constantly looking for opportunities to extend their learning and build a career platform that will maximise their opportunities in life. To do this they seek employers that provide them with the greatest opportunity to expand their skill set and maximise their earnings. They have no intention of working for the same employer forever; they do not want a single job for life. Employers must therefore invest in their people to ensure that they remain an employer of choice, with talented individuals clamouring to join their organisation, while at the same time delivering opportunities for progression for those already in the business to fulfil their future ambitions.

Herbert Meyer served during the Reagan administration as special assistant to the Director of the Central Intelligence Agency and Vice Chairman of the CIA's National Intelligence Council. In a global briefing to CEOs he presented an argument that the demographic of the vast majority of civilisation is changing dramatically – birth rates in many countries are falling below the sustainable population rate. If we accept Meyer's perception as valid, and add in that advances in medicine, health and social awareness are making people live longer, the result is that over the coming years, available skilled employees will become a scarcer commodity, with organisations seeking to employ individuals from an ever-decreasing candidate pool.

Globalisation forces organisations into common ways of working, not only to reap the financial opportunities that scale can provide but also to ensure that services are geared to the requirements of customers who have representation across more than one country – or indeed, continent.

Having global reach forces organisations to create operating structures that maximise performance in a manageable way. This has led to the emergence of hub, or continental organisation structures. Each is defined as a geographically knit business unit made up of a number of countries, all with their own in-market team but reporting to a regional centre – all the European countries, for example, reporting into a head office in Geneva. These individual countries will have their own local priorities but will all be striving to achieve performance targets associated with the global brands of the business.

Against any metric, insular ways of working in individual markets does not maximise performance. Take the recruitment, movement and promotion of people. Without common ways of working it is hard, if not impossible, to export talented individuals from one part of the organisation to another. In my early career, for example, I worked in an organisation that had a number of operating companies. To progress within that organisation I zigzagged through the business – a hotel manager in one part, an area manager in another, a divisional director in another. Each new role brought challenges, but a similarity in approach meant that my skill sets stayed relevant and were transferable across the broader organisation. Company-wide, such a global approach to skills development made it easier for the business to identify and nurture its future leadership.

So while a sales team has to be absolutely centred on offering propositions that are specifically tailored to the needs of their customers, there are significant financial, practical and technical advantages to fostering common ways of working.

- It increases employee loyalty.
- It minimises investment by having one way of working as opposed to a number.
- It ensures that there is a common way of measurement of peoples' skills and capabilities.
- It ensures that global customers recognise a common way of working locally.
- Most importantly, it allows businesses to foster a culture where there are opportunities for every employee to maximise their potential within the business.

Connecting a company's goal with those of teams and individuals is a must when creating solutions that will drive performance. So how do you create a common way of working within the sales arm of an organisation that minimises investment, can handle geographical and cultural boundaries as though they do not exist, while at the same time giving every person the autonomy and accountability for their own learning? The answer lies in three specific areas; a sales organisation where the route of all selling solutions lies in the needs of the customers; transitioning the role of sales managers to become the coaches and mentors of their teams; and crystalline clarity in fostering an environment where individuals are passionate about their personal learning and development.

In January 2005 I opened the doors of a new business, a very new chapter in my working life. Never before had I been the only person accountable for every single 'in' and every single 'out' on a profit and loss account. I had always had the support of fantastic brands or concepts, with a proven customer base fuelled by a host of consumers who already had a degree of loyalty to whatever product or service my employers were providing. Yes, there were always massive challenges to overcome and superb opportunities to exploit, but I was never before in a world where the rewards that I would receive, or salary I would draw, was so directly dependent on my own ability to produce profit and cash flow. The disciplines of running a business for which I was totally accountable, not to say reliant upon, focused my mind in the most intense way. Not only did I need to sell business to potential clients, but I also had to construct outstanding solutions for realising my clients' opportunities while managing the fledgling company that REL Sales Consulting was at that time.

Essential to building the business was being very clear on the areas in which we would specialise, and then exploiting every grain of experience I had accumulated to date. The additional skills and capabilities of contacts and colleagues ensured that we built solutions for clients that have become the backbone of our business and reputation.

To a degree I felt as if I were moving from being a gamekeeper to a poacher. I was well aware of the perception many people have of consultants going into businesses and replaying what they hear, borrowing your watch to tell you the time. Clear to me was that the world does not need any more consultants to go into organisations and tell them what to do.

Instead, we opted for a model where our clients' customers would come to be at the centre of any solution. We would focus on defining how our clients could outperform their competitors and grow market share. We would develop solutions based on the opportunities that our clients' customers had identified. Over time this has taken us down many avenues of opportunity, from the tools that are used within the business and the development of outstanding operating standards to how to identify and nurture talent. However, our aim, no matter what the content of a solution may be, is primarily concerned with embedding learning into the organisations with which we work. With learning embedded in the organisations they are able and motivated to take it forward and let it evolve with time.

This is where my passion really lies, embedding solutions as opposed to delivering solutions. To do this, we focus on energising a culture where the line managers within our clients' organisations are given the freedom, coaching and support to take accountability and responsibility for the development of their people. We never directly train members of a sales team. We minimise the investment required for external input by equipping the line managers within our clients' businesses with the skills and confidence to train their people. But there still remains a requirement to seek external input for a number of reasons.

- Understanding what good practice is in the broader commercial arena.
- Refreshing the skills of existing line managers.
- Developing individuals who are new to the role of managing a sales team.
- Creating new skills in line with the changing dynamics of business.

The fact is, that the level of retention and engagement of new skills and capabilities within sales teams is far higher, and has greater longevity, when they are coached within the organisation, as opposed to external people coming in to do the training and then leaving the team and individuals to interpret and demonstrate the skills for themselves.

In partnership with our clients we explore a world where the focus is on learning and not training; where learning is experiential, giving individuals the opportunity, through a combination of culture and methodologies, to embrace the ways of working within the organisation in a style that is relevant and appropriate for them.

Connecting a company's goals with those of teams and individuals is a must when creating solutions that will drive performance. After exploring how individual behaviour influences the performance of others, we look for effective ways of driving change in people's capability by connecting the brain with learning. We explore some solutions that connect the goals of a business to those of their teams and individual team members.

Solutions are never the same for every opportunity, but we have compiled an approach to the structuring, or packaging, of training material that, when applied effectively, will make organisations less reliant on external support by minimising corporate memory loss. We believe that over time you get what you measure. Having operating standards for teams is the first ingredient in determining their effectiveness.

In this book we will review those practices that are applicable to the world of sales, whether in a global organisation or a small local team supporting a fledgling business. We will then look at some of the ways in which we have applied some of the core skills of selling into a wide range of businesses.

Inspirational sales leadership lies at the heart of building a self-sufficient, high performing and sustainable sales team. To achieve this we will examine how to make managers into great coaches as well as great leaders.

> '*A book reads the better which is our own, and has been so long known to us, that we know the topography of its blots, and dog's ears, and can trace the dirt in it to having read it at tea with buttered muffins.*'
> **CHARLES LAMB, writer and essayist**

Learning is a personal experience. To assist you I have left some space for you to capture your own thoughts and learnings at the end of every chapter. I have recounted a few of my personal experiences, both good and bad. Please spend some time thinking of your own examples in the scenarios I describe, as this will create more meaning for you than only reading of my experiences. I would encourage you to personalise your learning by making notes in margins, using sticky notes or any other method that works for you. There is a page after each chapter to record any action plans you may formulate while you are thinking about how you can 'Turn your sales force into profit heroes'.

We will embark on a journey that will lead you to a new era where every person is not only passionate but also personally fulfilled through the performance of your organisation.

Part I

How to turn people into learners and heroes

ARE YOU RESPONSIBLE FOR THE WAY OTHERS BEHAVE?

There are two types of people: those who walk into a room and say, 'well, here I am' and those who walk into a room and say, 'ah, there you are'.

FREDERICK COLLINS, US lawyer and politician

Everyday we make choices. The biggest one is choosing our attitude. When I reflect on any of my relationships it is clear to me that the way that I behave is in some way mirrored by those with whom I come into contact. So, if I make the right choices as a husband, parent, friend, boss, peer or any other relationship, I will have a far more fulfilling and productive day.

In this chapter we will discover:

- how our behaviour influences those around us;
- how line management is about more than delivering a set of numbers;
- that line managers have to nurture as well as manage their people; and
- it takes time to coach.

Behave as though 'How we are is how others behave'

The ability and skills to guide individuals to perform better in their roles are perhaps the key characteristics that distinguish highly effective managers. Having the determination to achieve results throughout a team by developing their skills and behaviour provides a sound platform from which to drive profitable business performance. Yet the assessment of line managers, particularly those with profit and loss accountability for sales, is often more focused on the more tangible areas of measurement like deployment of sales teams, adherence to company strategy, successfully activating activity at the point of consumer or shopper purchase, achievement of targets and the identification of new channels of business as opposed to the primary focus being on the development of their teams.

Individuals working within teams would ideally look to their managers as role models: they seek individuals who have the experience and a real understanding of what they as salespeople are tasked with achieving on a day-to-day basis. They expect their manager to have a keen eye on developing the capability of each member of their team and, frankly, primarily themselves.

During some workshops I have used a very simple demonstration to try to get individuals to understand that how you behave is how others will behave as well. Well, almost!

Try out this simple exercise with a group:

While standing put your arm in the air making sure that your elbow is locked and your hand is pointing straight up to twelve o'clock. Then ask the group to do the same. When everyone has done it ask them to keep still and take a look around at each other. They will notice that probably none of them have got their hand straight up.

They will all have their arm raised but very few, if any, will be locked at the elbow. They have all got their hands up but none of them have done exactly the same as you, with directions drifting between 09:30 and 11:30 on a clock face. Later in the book we will take a look at how some people, who have inspired me on brain-based learning, have interpreted the context of this but for now we can realise that people do not do exactly what you demonstrate. The lesson is that if line managers are not driven, motivated and leading by example, how on earth can they expect teams reporting to them to be so?

In life we all assume different roles at different times. In the workplace this can include being a subordinate, a peer, a manager, a customer, a supplier and numerous others. Our roles extend even further outside our work place into being a friend, a son or daughter, a grandchild, a lover, a team mate and … the list goes on and on.

For me, becoming a parent was the one role through which I have discovered that actually the roles we have in life are not all that distinct and that good managers are ones who can learn from all their experiences in order to make themselves even better leaders of their teams.

The debate rages as to when is the ideal time to have a family. Perhaps those who have a family under thirty are more likely to engage with the social needs of their children. But if you are a bit more mature, you can share your worldly experiences and be potentially better equipped to provide for their ever-increasing thirst for knowledge – oh, and their financial demands. Is it easier to build a career if you have selflessly invested your time and energy to give your professional ambitions an early boost and postponed the family? The answer surely always rests in both the individual and their circumstances.

Having children later in life has been for me one of the most rewarding yet at the same time challenging things I have ever done. If I had benefited from all of the learning I have had in my first six years of parenthood, I know I would have been a better line manager. I would have spent more time understanding what lies behind individuals' behaviour, I would have been better at demonstrating the benefits of any of my actions and communications with the teams with whom I was working. I would definitely have been more selfless, and perhaps most importantly I would have taken far greater pride in seeing my team members develop their skills and behaviour, discovering for themselves what drives and motivates them as individuals.

It is, of course, sometimes me who is the cause of tension in my family life: this really hit home to me some time ago.

We were trying to leave the house for a family occasion and my two sons were taking their usual time to get ready with little sense of urgency. They were meandering with endless distractions that led their attention anywhere other than completing the job in hand.

My elder son was in the utility room attempting to clean his shoes with one of those wipe-on magic shoe cleaners. Yes, we have succumbed to taking the easier route rather than teaching the application of shoe polish! I went in to move the process along but found a scene of devastation. Everywhere was covered with a glistening sheen of freshly applied polish with precious little having made its way onto his shoes. I did not help. I talked sharply to him, telling him to wipe it off the floor and various other items, to start again and for the tenth time to hurry up.

After I had stormed off to the car my younger son went in to ask his brother to clean his shoes to which, unsurprisingly he received very short shrift. This ended with him running away wailing to his bedroom. Net result – the whole house was in uproar.

It could have all been so different. If I had stopped for a couple of minutes with my elder son and shown him how he could do a quicker and better job, and had been a little more supportive to his efforts, I could have avoided the ripple effect that engulfed our home.

I stood back and apologised to my son. He then (under his own steam) apologised to his brother. I learnt that 'How I am is how others behave'. Line managers need to nurture their teams providing support and guidance, but this only happens if the organisation sponsors a philosophy of 'My Line Manager Is My Coach and Mentor'.

Don't just check the numbers

In any walk of business, measurement of performance includes:

- Top line organic growth
- Cash flow
- Profitability
- Market share performance
- Innovation
- Cost of sales
- Connection with consumers
- Management of customers
- Sustainability.

Line managers are critical to success in all these areas, and many others too, with their superiors typically measuring performance by whether they deliver their numbers in whatever shape or form they may take.

When the going gets a little harder, which it always will do at some time or another – as evidenced by the economic climate in which the world finds itself in 2009 – it is not unusual for managers to revert to more direct management tactics, involving a culture of telling as opposed to coaching. Let's not forget the impact of telling someone to clean their shoes as opposed to coaching them on how to clean their shoes.

Building sustainable and mutually successful relationships with customers and consumers is the cornerstone of all successful businesses. It's the salespeople who speak most often to customers. Ensuring that they are motivated and equipped with the skills, knowledge and behaviour to outperform competitors and grow market share is a major determinant in driving sustainable business performance. To make this happen each and every day is down to ensuring that line managers operate in an environment where *how* they deliver their numbers is as crucial as the numbers that they deliver.

Nurture them as well as manage them

The origin of the word 'coach' comes from the village of Kocs in Hungary, where horse-drawn coaches were first made! In my business, the word coach refers to: *equipping line managers with the ability, motivation and skills to guide individuals to perform better in their roles in order to create excellent performance.*

In no way does this lead us down the path of advocating an environment where poor performance is addressed through reasoning and training. There will always be occasions where you have to make tough decisions and more senior individuals have to address 'people issues' personally.

My line management career started from what, some may say, is the bottom rung of a very long ladder. I worked in pub/restaurants as an assistant manager where I occasionally was in charge (well, that is how I defined it as a young man!). I moved on into hotel management, running groups of off-licences and managing divisions of large pub/restaurant operating companies. From this background in food and beverage retailing I had the opportunity of moving to the iconic brewing company, Guinness, who acquired my alcohol beverage retailing skills to manage an international pub virtual franchise business. Through this we assisted entrepreneurs, by applying six critical success criteria, to open outstanding pubs. The benefit to Guinness was that these outlets sold eighteen times more beer than an outlet that we had not assisted. After eighteen months I had the opportunity to extend my skills and knowledge into the very different world of being responsible for the total activity across a number of countries. A baptism of fire quickly ensued!

As a new general manager in Eastern Europe not long after the Russian financial crisis of August 1999 I was responsible for managing what was a growing, but suddenly coming under severe pressure, business exporting beer from Western Europe into countries such as Russia, Poland, Ukraine and indeed all of the ex-soviet states. I had individuals employed in various countries responsible for the day-to-day management of distributors and key customers.

A situation eventually arose in which a distributor owed us a considerable sum of money. They said they had the means to pay but had no way to transfer the funds to us. The local employee was not getting anywhere in collecting the monies and I felt that it fell to me to take direct action as opposed to coaching my salesperson in recovering debt.

After lengthy consultations with my boss and the group's central security team we agreed that I should be the one to go and attempt to recover the debt owed to the business. So I left London and was met in Kiev by an armed bodyguard, escorted to a hotel overnight, with the bodyguard setting up camp in the room next to me. Me and my shadow then visited the distributor the next morning and after a brief meeting they provided us with the funds and I was then escorted back to the airport. On returning to London the funds were duly deposited in the bank. My immediate thought was that I'd done a great job, my only regret being that I'd flown back to London on the same plane that my favourite football team, Arsenal, had arrived on to play a Champions League game against Dynamo Kiev the next evening.

The experience of debt collection from the Ukraine was neither pleasant nor clever, but I had addressed the business need. However, on mature reflection, I realised that Darek, the salesperson, had been left behind with the empty feeling that he had failed to do the job of managing the distributor that was needed.

I received accolades from my boss and peers, yet in all reality it felt a bit hollow. I had forgotten one crucial thing. I had done this myself as opposed to working through my team. While it was possible to count the cash it was not possible to measure the dent in my team member's morale, or his very personal belief that he was not doing a great job for the organisation. I owe Darek a very belated apology.

So yes, there are times when line managers need to take direct action for the good of the business, but understanding the consequences of direct management action as opposed to nurturing and coaching the capability of people is crucial. You have to find a balance. A rationale and some positioning involvement, in the instance of Darek, would have provided for a win–win outcome. Guinness would have received the money that they were owed and the salesperson would have understood how he could approach a similar situation slightly differently in the future and enjoy some of the kudos of success.

Take the time to coach

My youngest son is currently learning the art of putting on his own shoes. However, whenever we are in a hurry I catch myself reverting to the old way: I put the shoes on for him with the net result of getting out of the door considerably more quickly. If I were to practise my coaching beliefs, in my role as a dad, by supporting his endeavours to put his shoes on instead of bypassing his learning to meet my immediate needs he would be self-sufficient a lot quicker.

To overcome this depends on timing. This means getting ready to leave five minutes earlier or coaching the salesperson in how to recover the debt before it becomes business-critical. The benefits of both of these adages would have been the same, i.e. the shoes would be on and the money in the bank. The one exception being that either my son or Darek would have been far better equipped to tackle the situation for themselves in the future if I had coached them rather than done the task for them.

The impact of the example from the Ukraine was that I had not coached Darek in how to effectively manage the distributor around the issue of collecting debt. Did we have our money? Well, yes we did. Did Darek now know how he could have managed the situation more effectively? Well, probably not; and it is no coincidence to me that I found myself a few months later having to recruit a new person in the Ukraine. Was this a result of Darek feeling undermined in his role? That may be a bit extreme, as the working environment at that time was intolerably tough, but I do think it is reasonable to suggest that my management style on the issue of debt recovery did little to suggest to him that the business we were both working for was a place where he could develop his personal capability under a supportive line manager who was sensitive to his development needs.

As we create an environment where line managers are empowered to drive the growth of their areas of responsibility, we will discover some hints, tips and techniques to make lasting change in the effectiveness of this crucial population within any business. We will examine some ways to make the organisation less reliant on individuals by having the tools and methods to ensure that corporate memory loss does not become a block for future business growth. We have to learn from experience and keep that learning in the organisation. We will minimise the gap between what is and what could be by everyone embracing the adage of My Line Manager is My Coach and Mentor.

An early lesson is to always remember that we will only get out of our relationships what we are prepared to put into them. This means that line managers must take a proactive role in building the skills and capabilities of their teams. So the answer to building highly skilled and effective teams does not rest on having personal reviews with team members to identify skills gaps and then sending people on either internal or external courses. There's more to it than that.

The secret to success rests in making line managers passionate about developing their teams themselves; it's about equipping them with the tools and methodology to improve the skills of their teams through daily coaching. It is then the organisation's responsibility to recognise that the traditional measures of line mangers are not enough. The priority is to measure how highly people development is regarded, and reward and recognise those that reward and recognise the skills and commitment of their teams.

Unlike the advances in technology where we have access to instant communication, there are no short cuts when it comes to instilling within an organisation an environment where line managers are personally motivated and measured on how they pursue lasting capability change within their team. As I write this I have just received an e-mail that reads as follows:

Hi Peter,
I still have positive memories from the training you and
your colleague did with us. The training was about having
interactive workshops. With my new team we have started
a big change programme in order to globally improve
the competencies in distribution and logistics. We have

*experimented a bit with the REL style interactive work-
shops and this was very positive. In order to fully equip my
full team (9 people) with the competence to have such an
interactive workshop I am looking for a similar training as
we had with the Commercial and Sales Development team.
It would be good to hear from you.
Kind regards,
Rafael*

English is not Rafael's first language but we can see that embracing
the methodology of effective training to create maximum engagement,
retention and recall is dear to his heart. He continues to use the methodology he discovered through one of our workshops some three years
ago.

Embracing a systematic approach where individuals drive capability for themselves has a lasting effect as we can see from Rafael's
note. It ensures that skills and knowledge can become a key part of a
line manager's toolkit. Quite clearly Rafael realises that how he and
his team are interacting between themselves and others is critical to
getting others within his organisation to adopt whatever messages
they are trying to cascade.

So from my experience it is clear that you are responsible for how
others behave. If a line manager is not 100% committed to building
the capability of his team he cannot expect it to be done for him by others, or blame individuals within his team who are falling below whatever the required standards may be. Members of any team need to
feel nurtured and inspired by their boss. Line mangers must reinforce
learning needs at every juncture and be committed to developing their
people through the application of tools and techniques that create a
common methodology of execution across the organisation.

Success is then much more than purely numbers. As well as the
brands, route to market, pricing and all other business fundamentals,
great numbers are just as much a by-product of a high-performing
team. It makes sense measuring line managers on their ability to develop a talented team as well as delivering the traditional financial
measurements.

Key learnings	That's interesting

Action plan	
What could I do?	
Who would it involve?	
When should I aim to have it done by?	
What resources or dependencies are involved?	

CONNECTING THE BRAIN WITH BUILDING CAPABILITY

'Men wanted: for hazardous journey. Small wages, bitter cold, long months of complete darkness, constant danger, safe return doubtful. Honour and recognition in case of success.'

SIR ERNEST SHACKLETON,
explorer

Why will 75% of what you plan to change within your organisation never happen? There is a multitude of answers to this; however, the key one is PEOPLE. Most adults have little knowledge of effective learning techniques, so the perception that training is what builds capability is widely held. In my experience learning is actually what differentiates people; the distinction being that training is done 'to' people as opposed to learning which is done by themselves.

In this chapter we will discover:

- why we learn in differing ways;
- an example of cascading training;
- how to ensure that line managers and their training material appeal to all styles of learning; and
- the attributes of a stimulating learning environment.

Throughout our education we commonly underwent similar experiences to our peers – lectures, practical experiences or tasks to complete through home study. However, it is obvious that we all achieved differing results. We attribute that to varying levels of application, our ability to digest information that we can recall in a given context, our drive and determination to study and many other factors.

As an individual I had what could be classified as a fairly common UK education. I did OK but would not be classified as an outstanding scholar – more in the middle of the pack. As a child I really enjoyed physical team sport activities, and learned to play a number of musical instruments. Reading and writing poetry was something I also did.

When studying for A levels I was often looking for excuses to get out of late afternoon classes on a Monday, Wednesday and Friday, in order to get to the local dog racing track. I was working there as a waiter in the restaurant and then, after a short while, actually managing the operation. I was learning how to delight customers, how to influence those working with me and how to build great relationships. Most importantly I was watching and listening how others, more experienced than me, practised their trade. I was learning through doing as opposed to learning through reading, group education or listening to lectures.

After my A levels I had choices about where to continue my studies. I was offered opportunities at various places, but while contemplating which curriculum aroused my passion the most, I found myself writing over forty application letters to various employers in the food and beverage industry around the UK. I had a longing to extend my learning through doing as opposed to sitting and listening. Life is full of choices, and at that stage I decided to accept one of the two offers that I received from all those letters of application. We all have the ability to forge our future if we have the determination and perseverance to do so.

Find out how people learn

I never really understood my approach to learning; yes, I participated in education but it never really stimulated me and as a result I guess initially I did not demonstrate my full potential.

There are times in life when someone turns the light bulb on. One such occasion was when I was metaphorically introduced to Howard Gardner, who I have come to realise is an educational genius. Gardner was born in Pennsylvania in 1943 and is a psychologist and Professor of Cognition and Education at Harvard. He has also written in excess of twenty books that have been translated and reprinted many times over. In his book *Frames of Mind* (Basic Books 1983), Gardner determined that intelligence is a compound of various types of intelligences. What this meant to me was that we all learn in different ways. Gardner identified that there are eight primary ways in which people learn and that we all have differing preferences. Here are these intelligences, or styles.

- Linguistic – using words, both written and spoken.
- Logical/Mathematical – working through in a structured fashion.
- Visual/Spatial – needing to see what something looks like.
- Musical – putting things to rhyme or music for easy recall.
- Kinaesthetic/Bodily – moving to action with physical experimentation.
- Interpersonal – working with others in groups.
- Intrapersonal – having time to reflect and study on your own.
- Naturalistic – observing, practising and communing.

When I stood back and reflected on my personal learning preferences I realised that they probably did not lie in those that were commonly used in the education I received at school. There was lots of classroom work (interpersonal); in my mind, too much homework (intrapersonal); and an over-reliance on linguistic learning.

It was no surprise to discover that my primary personal learning preferences lay in visual/spatial, kinaesthetic/bodily and linguistic. So I guess that could be a reason why I did OK as opposed to demonstrating my true capability at the early stages of my education. There was no direct relation between how I was being taught and how I could maximise my learning.

I was introduced to Gardner's thinking when I was part of a team responsible for both the authoring and embedding of the initial components of a sales skills programme at Diageo, which Paul Walsh has identified in his foreword as 'The Diageo Way of Selling'. The team and I realised that the development of such things as sales operating standards, a common approach to a structured call or any other skills or tools application were not enough to bring them to life within a global sales team. It was very evident that it was not only about creating 'best in class' training materials but also about the way in which they were 'cascaded' to sales teams to ensure that a common way of selling was established across the organisation.

Through experience and evaluation we learn what works and what we can improve on. By working with various customers, we have developed training materials to create 'best in class' for sales teams. We will examine the components of achieving this across a number of chapters; however, the first point is about making the materials relevant to any learners. This initially means packaging material in such a way that gives individuals the very best chance of understanding it, and then of adopting the topics of learning, ultimately to create a common way of selling across every team in every part of the organisation.

Within this global sales team, we engaged the support of learning experts who introduced us to a very new world centred upon putting the spotlight on the learners instead of ourselves. They taught us how to make meaningful learning experiences and shared with us a huge number of hints and tips to turn our raw educational materials into something far more stimulating and useful for learners. Applying Gardner's thinking was critical for us to create experiences that would hold resonances with any and all of our learners.

The secret of embedding learning is to connect the brain with building capability. Learners have to be able to clearly see how any given topic will improve their personal capability. The experience of learning has to be enjoyable and rewarding. However, to achieve this consistently extends a long way beyond being cognisant of and applying Gardner's theories on multiple intelligences. On any journey to building capability, it is as much the 'how' you embed learning as the 'what' you are trying to embed that will determine the effectiveness of a team.

Train the trainers and the managers can train their people

I'm not sure who said 'copy everything I do apart from my mistakes', but I've found it useful. Partly with this in mind my approach to embedding learning is now constructed of a number of factors, the first of which is, that you need a framework of tools and skills. To develop these, start with a very clear set of operating standards that you are looking for a team to exhibit. We will examine a set of capability standards and how these are applied through skills and tools in later chapters; however, for now let's concentrate on how you bring them to life for learners by connecting the brain to building capability.

In 2006 I met the commercial director of an international brewing giant, who explained to me a significant challenge that they faced within their organisation. In Eastern Europe they employed a team of three thousand salespeople. They worked on different brands, spoke a multitude of differing languages and had numerous different ways of selling. It was becoming impossible to export talented individuals from one operating company to another. This was significantly limiting their potential to have common development platforms and, therefore effective succession planning, within the business. Senior managers, who were not working to a common organisational framework, were directing line managers each in their own particular way. In other words, there was no common way of selling.

So the challenge before us was, how do we embed a common way of selling within such a multi-faceted business? The solution was certainly not simply in the creation of new tools, systems or standards. They did not become one of the biggest brewers in the world based on a stack of cards. The solution lay in developing a culture where line managers were equipped with the ability to take responsibility for the development and success of their own teams while putting into place a common way of working that extended across the whole of the region.

Our first step was to gather a group of 'owners of content'. These were functional experts who were commonly tasked with developing solutions that ensured that they would outperform their competitors and grow market share. Representatives from the various countries joined them to determine the shape and construct of the skills, knowledge and behaviours they were seeking to embed. Once we had determined what the operating standards needed to be to create an outstanding sales organisation, we turned our focus onto the learners.

Working together we developed what was described as a 'Master Trainers' framework. What this meant was that a number of individuals across the organisation, regardless of their functional area, would be trained to train others in a common way.

We packaged content into bite-sized modules. We will take a look at how to do this a little later on. Then, crucially, we focused our energies on ensuring that this Master Trainer population truly understood how to make any learning session invigorating for all of their audiences. We created three-day sessions for building the awareness and skills of this vital Master Trainer population. These sessions focused primarily on creating an environment in which the learners would love to learn. We explored the attributes and methodologies to create maximum engagement, retention and recall with only about 20% of the three days focusing on the actual content that we were seeking to embed across the organisation. From there they would embark on a journey of cascading this approach to a population of almost four hundred, whose function could be described as area managers. They would then embrace the learning techniques to develop their teams – the three thousand salespeople.

Ensure that line managers and their training material appeal to all styles of learning

So how do you create an awareness of the most effective ways in which to engage learners, to ensure that content is retained and recalled when you are working with customers from the furthest reaches of the Asian part of Russia to ultra-European Vienna?

I have been on a journey, through coaching from learning experts, working with colleagues, and application with customers, to discover that there are eight key ingredients beyond the content itself to creating an experience that will stimulate learners. We can summarise these as follows.

1   Focusing on the needs of learners.
2   Taking one step at a time.
3   Creating a love and space for learning.
4   Using inclusive language while exhibiting the right behaviours.
5   Recognising that we all learn subconsciously.
6   Recognising that people enter learning with different levels of skill.
7   Managing the learning environment.
8   The use of permanent messages.

Using these guidelines it becomes possible to influence what lies behind performance, whether they are situational, motivational, experiential and temperamental, or skill factors.

Therefore, in packaging any learning experience we look to construct any session behind these eight beliefs, and when supplemented by the creation of materials and contents that embrace all of Gardner's primary intelligences you start to connect the brain directly with building capability.

It makes sense then, to examine what lies behind the eight ingredients.

1 Focusing on the needs of learners

'I like to do all the talking myself. It saves time,
and prevents arguments.'
                    OSCAR WILDE, playwright, poet and wit

Trainers are a bit like visual aids on a screen; one minute they are there and the next they are gone. The result is that learners know they saw something but are not necessarily able to recall what they saw, let alone put into practice what it was hoped they would have learnt. By ensuring that focus is firmly deflected away from the trainer and onto the learner encourages an environment of participation and experiential learning. Remember that learning is what people do for themselves, while training is done to someone.

There are a number of things that, it would not be exaggerating to say, I have come to despise in training sessions I have attended in the past. I really don't like people being asked to introduce themselves. You sit in a room and everyone is asked to introduce themselves, and even being asked to tell the other members of the group something that the others did not know about them. Often, the people attending programmes already know each other – so what is the purpose? Well, for a trainer it gives them the chance to hear everyone's name. What is the relevance for the learner? Something close to zero. People only half listen at best to those who stand before them; the trepidation increases for those who have to introduce themselves later, and they concentrate on preparing to say something wittier than the last person.

So what this means in a learning environment is that in order to focus on the needs of the learners, the trainer has to take responsibility that everything said and handed out is relevant, and packaged in such a way that appeals to varying styles of intelligence or learning. The more a trainer is able to stand back and allow learners to step out of the shadows and lead the learning experience, the better the chance of the subject living within the person and the organisation long after the session.

A line manager leading the learning and reinforcing the required behaviour on a day-to-day basis through coaching, supplements the effectiveness of the material. The results can be startling compared with traditional course attendance.

We use very simple tools to ensure that we are considering the needs of learners in any session that we deliver. The most relevant of all is taking the time to develop detailed session plans which focus on five key areas.

- What the bite-size piece of content is.
- The timing of each session.
- What the trainer is doing and saying.
- What resources are needed.
- Critically, what the learners are going to do during the session.

2   Taking one step at a time

> 'How time flies when you's doin' all the talking.'
> **HARVEY FIERSTEIN, actor and writer**

Any trainer has an absolute responsibility to ensure that any learning session is well structured, is as easy as possible to follow and is totally relevant. A learning experience is about coaching new skills, knowledge and behaviour. It is not a test to see how readily attendees can recall a complex set of tasks. How often have you been in a group where someone has reeled off a series of rapid instructions? For example:

> 'We are now going to do a breakout exercise that will last twenty-five minutes. Get into groups of three making sure you don't get into a group with people you have worked with today. The task is to identify the attributes of a highly

effective team, how to recognise success and what are the best ways of ensuring that their success is communicated broadly across the organisation. Collect flip chart paper and pens from the front desk. Head off to anywhere you feel comfortable not forgetting to let me know where you are going first. Once in your group ensure that you have identified a group leader, a scribe and the other person will then share the outputs from the session you are about to have. Right, I will see you back in this room in twenty-five minutes from now.'

Stop and think for a minute. What is the impact of this style of communication on a learner? For me it creates complete confusion. There is a multitude of tasks to take in all at once. Precious few of which have got anything to do with the actual learning experience.

The trainer's responsibility is to brief actions clearly and most importantly, one step at a time, providing learners with the resources to support them in completing the session to the very best of their potential. This ensures that the learning is structured, has meaning and ultimately enhances retention and recall when outside of the learning environment.

3　Creating a love and space for learning

'Fine jade is produced out of ugly stone. People of talent are produced through training and development.'

Chinese proverb

As we have realised from Gardner's teachings we all learn at differing speeds and in different ways, so it is crucial to ensure that we appeal to the preferred ways of learning of all the learners. This can be summarised as creating the environment, mechanics and time for each participant to get the most value out of the experience. We will be taking a look into materials a little later on; however, spending some time in understanding environmental issues at this stage will make sure that we have an inclusive learning arena.

A number of physical factors are important such as natural light, space and informal seating arrangements. Then we must give learners choices on how they will best absorb the content. Choices are brought to life in several areas – having learner notebooks where participants can personalise what they have learnt, using options for extending their learning after a session; electronic learning tools and suggested reading lists are good examples. Now add in a mixture of learning styles, such as group working and working in pairs. Physical activity, like working on an exercise from a poster is a superb way to appeal to varying learning styles and it also has a dramatic impact in energising the environment.

In the piece of work with the brewing giant, our focus in developing the session was on the learners and not on just cascading a whole load of content to them. We made sure that the training had real relevance for them, and we constantly supported their learning journey through pre-exposure to the content and reinforcement after the sessions were completed.

Learning should be an enjoyable experience for everyone involved, the goal being that everyone is energised and looking forward to the next learning experience, realising the benefits they will get from it.

4 Using inclusive language while exhibiting the right behaviours

'How often misused words generate misleading thoughts.'
HERBERT SPENCER, biologist and philosopher

The most productive weapon in any trainer's armoury is language. Obviously in sessions that include individuals from varying nationalities it is important that language is simple and easy to follow with jargon completely outlawed.

All trainers must be enthusiastic, committed and fully involved with any learning interaction. You will recall in chapter one I wrote about the simple exercise of putting your hand in the air and asking a group to copy you. The learning we derived from examining that very simple exercise is that at best you will only get back from people fifty plus per cent of what you put in yourself. If a trainer is not passionate and committed, demonstrating infectious enthusiasm how can we expect others to behave in that way?

The language that we use is also about inclusivity. This is a journey that everyone in the room is undertaking together. Using words and phrases like 'we', 'together', 'follow me into a new experience', 'wouldn't it be great', all provide a visible belief of a shared learning environment.

It is not what we are trying to do, but how we do it that will lead to great results. If we examine the monologue we looked at under *'Taking one step at a time'* we can find some clues. As well as breaking the instructions down into individual components that the group can follow one after another, demonstration or modelling behaviour is also really important. By way of a simple explanation of the point, let's for one moment examine the briefing for collecting the pens and flip chart paper. If as a trainer we walk over to the items and pick them up ourselves while briefing the activity, the learners both see and hear the required activity. Such modelling actions are really helpful in supplementing the language that we use.

5 *Recognising that we all learn subconsciously*

> '*Without experiencing a thing, one cannot grow in knowledge. Wisdom comes from experience.*'
>
> **Chinese proverb**

Why do organisations spend millions of pounds on advertising campaigns? Why do they encourage us to sample new products? Why do we get stacks of junk mail through the door? It's obvious really; companies are trying to get us as consumers to purchase their products, encourage us to try new things and experiences.

In life though, through research we know that over ninety per cent of what we learn has happened subconsciously. It is always quicker to get through an airport the third or fourth time than it is the first or second. Why is that? Well, we know the best entry doors, we have an idea of our check-in area, we do not spend ages with our heads in the air trying to fathom out which way we need to walk towards our boarding gate or where the nearest toilets are. We have learnt our way round. We do not do this consciously, thinking that we need to make sure we learn the layout of this airport so that our journey through is quicker next time. We learn it through experience.

Learning everyday through experience means that a surprisingly small amount of what we learn is through what we are told, in a training arena or in our everyday lives. Our brains are absorbing information and lessons continually, without us even realising that we are learning.

Whenever we step into the role of trainer we can influence this process by ensuring that we create an environment where things are experiential, and learners are able to open their senses to the messages that the training is seeking to embed. Learning will always be a mixture of experiences, and it falls to the trainers to be aware that there is a huge benefit in tapping into the subconscious through all the methods available to them. We have already discovered some of these with such things as learning activities, role-play, experiential learning, visual messages and both intrapersonal and interpersonal learning.

6   Recognising that people enter learning with different levels of skill

'Got up. Shaved. Had breakfast. Did the Times *crossword. Had another shave.'*
ARTHUR SMITH, humourist and stand up comedian

Organisations recruit people with different levels of skills and experience. People change their functional role within a business; they get a promotion or even move to a different site or country. The effect of this is that every member of a team or group enters into learning with different levels of both knowledge and experience.

We need to recognise this, but also ensure that any learning experience involves complete participation from everyone. The learning journey should always end up with everyone experiencing the same, regardless of their knowledge or expertise. This is important in creating a common way of working, with all the benefits that this will bring. Nevertheless, learning becomes even more powerful for a group when a trainer can encourage members of the group to share their knowledge and experiences, demonstrating real situational relevance.

A learning session should always have a very clear purpose: 'by the end of this session we will …'. I was some time ago discussing the principles of anchoring a learning. This was not something new to me, but the context I found really helpful. The word 'anchoring' brings to my mind big ships sitting outside a harbour, not going anywhere but secured to the spot. The principles of anchoring in learning for me are quite similar to this analogy. When running an exercise, delivering a piece in plenary or for that matter any chunk of learning it is beneficial to the learners if you not only say what you are going to cover, but then at the end summarise the key points by perhaps using a poster or by asking learners to reflect on what they have learnt.

7 *Managing the learning environment*

> *'Close to the mountains there is more rain; close to the sea there is more wind. One is always influenced by one's surroundings.'*
>
> **Chinese proverb**

I know many people who, like me, are dispirited at the thought of sitting through an all-day meeting. This is not normally because of the subject matter or the people in the meeting; it is more to do with the thought of sitting down for hours on end, being restricted by a table in front of me with others around me doing exactly the same thing.

If you are not already doing so, sit yourself down for a moment and have a think about your body. If you maintain the same position for twenty-five minutes or more, what has been happening to you? I am no physician but it is obvious to me that the blood in our bodies is around our knees and ankles and that through sitting down for extended periods of time we are reducing the flow of oxygenated blood to our brain. The result is that we absorb less information.

When running sessions I try to have lots of breaks. They may be only for five minutes at a time but they break up the learning into bite-sized chunks; and they also get learners to stand up and move away from the learning environment. There are many other ways to do the same thing. You can move the group to a different area of the room ('It would be great if you could join me at the back of the room as I have something on the wall I think you will really enjoy discovering, to emphasise this point'). You could run a brainstorming session. You could get the group into couples or trios, and ask them to go for a walk for three minutes to discuss their learnings from the last session. Just by changing the physicality of the environment we are giving learning such a better chance of being effective.

8   The use of permanent messages

'Research suggests that some learners pick up 80–85% of their key learning from visuals and posters mounted on the wall.'

TIM ANDREWS, founder Stretch Learning

In focusing on the needs of learners I referred to computer-generated visual support tools that appear on a screen. Think for one moment how long a slide stays projected onto a screen on average – thirty seconds, a minute, three? Regardless of the time it is there one moment and then it is gone. I think this is what has led me to despise all-day meetings. You often end up with a beauty parade of presentations with charts, diagrams, tools, processes and the like being thrown up on the screen in front of you. You barely manage to read all of the words – let alone hear what the presenter has to say about them. As to recalling the detail of a chart I had seen twenty slides ago or two hours ago, I would have zero chance of being able to recall the content anything like one hundred per cent accurately.

That's why in training, there is a huge relevance in decorating your environment with permanent messages. We use lots and lots of posters whenever we run an engagement or learning session. They do not have to have an obvious meaning, indeed far from it. They can sit on the wall often at an angle, as this forces learners to tilt their head giving that oxygenated blood another chance to stimulate the brain. Posters stay there for the whole session; they do not whizz on and off a screen at the click of a mouse. They are constantly reinforcing the key points of the learning. By using posters you are opening up individuals' minds to learning. They are wondering what a poster is trying to say. We use loads of hand-drawn visuals or even, if language is not a barrier to the group, cryptic messages such as using a space in w**ds for learners to fill in the gaps in their own minds. It is important though that you anchor any posters that you have put up by the end of any session. They should be massively relevant to a learning experience.

With practice we have found that it is possible to run a two-and-a-half-day session without using a single projected visual aid. We know that there is huge power in using peripheral messages that stay there for the whole time and reinforce the key components of a learning session.

When the eight components come together, learning can be such fun. Yes, it is hard work to embed a common approach to any capability programme, but when people's brains are so engaged with the learning and when they have the opportunity to explore the content at their own pace in their preferred styles of learning, the results are quite remarkable.

Building a company-wide capability standard can be a hazardous journey; you are not able to guarantee that it survives through training alone however, to use Sir Ernest Shackleton's quote, there is definitely honour and recognition in the event of success.

Key learnings	That's interesting

Action plan	
What could I do?	
Who would it involve?	
When should I aim to have it done by?	
What resources or dependencies are involved?	

WHAT'S IN IT FOR THE ORGANISATION?

3

'The difference between involvement
and commitment is best represented
when looking at your cooked breakfast.
A chicken was involved yet the pig was
fully committed.'

Anon

T he benefit to the organisation is central to any business activity. Estimating return on investment is a common barometer to establish how effective or efficient an investment could be. Equally, a robust process of measurement and evaluation after the implementation of an initiative can provide crucial learnings to establish the benefits of repeating a similar process or activity in the future.

When measuring the benefit of a tangible activity; for example, a new product launch, or perhaps a consumer loyalty activity at the point of purchase, there are clear measures of success. These metrics can include calculating how many more products have been sold, looking at the profitability of an activity and many other criteria.

Measuring the benefit of focusing on the development and training of a sales team is somewhat less tangible. Yes, you can look at retention statistics, performance of teams against common key performance indicators and achievement of individual development goals and sales statistics; for us however, structured feedback from all customers provides the real indicators of value in striving for world-class capability in selling.

In this chapter we will examine a model to define the benefit of embedding a common way of selling and training where line managers take accountability and responsibility for the development of their teams – being fully committed and not just involved in the nurturing of their people.

What's in it for me?

'I told you I was ill.'

SPIKE MILLIGAN's epitaph

Working within the sales arm of an organisation can be seen, as Paul Walsh has identified in the foreword to this book, as unglamorous, tactical, downstream, un-strategic and easy. These are perceptions held by others who have not been stimulated and motivated by being accountable for the key ingredient of success for any business – helping people to buy things. Without sales there is no revenue, without revenue there cannot be any profit and without profit, simply put, there is no business. It is therefore correct to assess that the sales team is in fact the cornerstone of any successful organisation. A range of specialist functions then support and fuel their efforts.

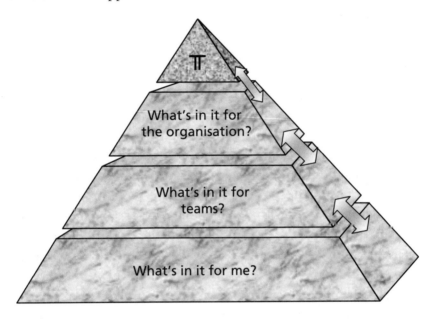

Most people have an inherent desire to be successful. No one can be successful on their own. They need to be inspired, coached and developed by leaders who have a passion and flair for seeing their teams excel in any competitive or commercial arena.

Since time began, humanity's inherent need for simple basics like food, heat and shelter has not been universally fulfilled. In the twenty-first century this is sadly still the case, with a significant proportion of the global population suffering from a lack of these staples of life. However, in the developed world of modern business, individuals look for far more from life beyond these three basic needs. This is not about greed, being seen to outperform their peer group or simply about accumulating wealth – it is about wanting to be fulfilled, a metric which varies for every person.

When working in an organisation there are a number of basic measures associated with 'what's in it for me' beyond the provision of the basic staples of life. These include:

- personal recognition
- remuneration
- career progression
- achieving objectives
- having fun
- having the opportunity to enjoy today
- working within an appealing culture.

Unlocking a sales team's inner strength means creating a firm affiliation between the needs of individuals and teams, and then connecting the goals that a team strives to achieve with those of the organisation.

In chapter five we will examine some of the foundation skills required to sell exceptional brands. One key component is to clearly and concisely identify the needs of customers; and here is our approach to building this capability with an organisation. You can apply the same principle to employees within any business. Identifying common drivers and motivators assists line managers to identify and articulate the benefits of a common approach to selling for the individual members of their teams.

Moreover, the benefits of understanding the needs of customers then extend to more tangible aspects for individuals. Here are these team member benefits.

- Having transferable skill sets which will allow them to foster their career ambitions.
- Being connected to the organisation and their peer group – one vision, one goal, one team.
- Being equipped to maximise their performance against their objectives providing enhanced recognition, rewards and opportunities for progression.

- Being able to interact with any type of customer, team member or internal support function in a way that provides for consistent mutual benefits. Simply put, creating amazing relationships.

Sales teams working within an environment where common ways of working and best demonstrated practice have been adopted, and who are trained and coached by passionate, knowledgeable and engaging line managers will ensure that they are equipped to outperform competitors and grow market share for the organisation.

As the young manager of a food and beverage retail outlet, I recall a particular area manager. His name was Patrick McGuire and was without doubt the most passionate line manager I have ever had the pleasure of working for. He would turn up in my restaurant at 10 p.m. on a Saturday night and pay a visit on Christmas Day morning; he was there with me and my team, not just acting as a figurehead. His standards were exacting and occasionally his demands became really tough. He was striving for excellence in every aspect of the business. This started with basics. He, rightly, had a fixation with weeds outside buildings. He would pull up the tiniest shoot, lecturing that a weed on the outside of a building made customers suspect that the kitchen was dirty. To this day I cannot walk past a weed on my drive without giving it a tug. His passion, energy and commitment were infectious, and what's more they embedded a change in standards in his team. Excellence became a habit, not a task.

Habits are hard to break. The identification and recognition of the benefits to individuals is a crucial first step into unlocking the commitment of every member of a team. Line managers have to be equipped to turn basic sales skills into sales habits.

Stephen Covey has written and lectured on the seven habits of highly effective people. These can be interpreted as being:

Habit 1 – 'proactive' ®

This is the ability to control one's environment, rather than have it control you, as is so often the case. It concerns self-determination, choice and the power to decide response to stimuli, conditions and circumstances.

Habit 2 – 'begin with the end in mind'

Personal leadership – means leading yourself towards what you consider your aims to be. By developing the habit of concentrating on relevant activities you will build a platform that avoids distractions and become more productive and successful.

Habit 3 – 'put first things first'

Personal management is about organising and implementing activities in line with the aims established in habit 2.

Habit 4 – 'think win–win'

Interpersonal leadership is necessary because achievements are largely dependent on co-operative efforts with others. Win–win is based on the assumption that there is plenty for everyone, and that success follows a co-operative approach more naturally than the confrontation of win-or-lose.

Habit 5 – 'seek first to understand and then to be understood'

Communication, 'diagnose before you prescribe' is simple, effective and essential for developing and maintaining positive relationships in all aspects of life.

Habit 6 – 'synergize'®

Creative co-operation – this is the principle that the whole is greater than the sum of its parts; it implies the challenge to see the good and potential in other peoples' contribution.

Habit 7 – 'sharpen the saw'®

This is self-renewal and necessarily surrounds all the other habits, enabling and encouraging them to happen and grow. There are four parts: the spiritual, mental, physical and the social/emotional, which all need feeding and developing.

Covey's teachings show us that there are a significant number of areas that organisations need to focus on to create a business and cultural environment within which individuals will thrive. To a certain degree these will vary depending on the business environment and the role an individual performs. However, being able to identify 'What's in it for me?' is a pivotal step in embedding a standard way of selling, and then reaping the benefits for teams and ultimately the organisation.

Talented and driven individuals choose organisations, not vice versa.

What's in it for teams?

> 'Even while they teach, men learn.'
>
> **SENECA ('THE YOUNGER'),**
> **Roman philosopher and poet**

The definition of the word 'team' is: a group of people organised to work together. Two of the words in this definition encapsulate *winning* teams: organised and together.

Sales teams are generally structured around two scenarios. The first is a geographical territory; and the second, a group of customers with similar needs or similar scale. These combinations of operating structures dictate that members of the team require a common approach or way of working. Having different ways of working and interaction with customers limits the achievements of a team.

In today's world an individual works for approximately 230 days per year, yet modern retail practice means that customers are trading nearly every day of the year. Selling is as much a reactive process as it is proactive. Subsequently, being able to react swiftly to customers' needs while identifying and addressing business opportunities as they emerge, requires team members to be able to spend time in the territory of colleagues. To maximise performance with customers it is essential that differing ways of working or communicating do not become an obstacle to exploiting an opportunity.

The one thing that can be guaranteed is that every member of a team will, at some stage, leave that team. Having a common way of operating will ensure the following.

- The performance of a team is not reliant on the performance of individuals.
- Customers see the same quality of interaction with the organisation no matter which individual they deal with.
- Providing that there is robust succession planning, there will not be a dip in performance of a territory when an incumbent salesperson moves on.

The role of sales leadership is to recognise the contribution of teams as much as it is to recognise the performance and potential of individuals.

In the world of motor sport, prizes are awarded for constructors as well as for individuals. Recognising that success comes collectively and is not purely something delivered by an individual ensures that everyone is striving towards a common goal, whether that is winning a constructors' championship or surpassing a sales team's annual operating plan.

Sales teams are not just the local territory team. Line managers are part of a team, often under the guidance and management of a regional director and the regional director – a sales leadership team. Each of these entities is as important as each other. They will ensure that through coaching and inspirational leadership there is a common commitment to achieving the required performance – one team, one vision, one goal.

What's in it for the organisation?

'In the business world, an executive knows something about everything, a technician knows everything about something, and the switchboard operator knows everything.'
HAROLD COFFIN, American humour columnist

In the introduction I outlined five key benefits to an organisation that fosters an environment where line managers transcend to the role of enthused and skilled coaches of their teams.

1   It increases employee loyalty

Individuals recognise and thrive in an environment where they are developing in a culture that they enjoy. They have pride and passion around the business and recognise the company as a place where they can have the opportunity to realise their short-, medium- and long-term career ambitions.

2   It minimises investment by having a single way of working

Creating revenue and converting it into profit is hard enough without various areas of the organisation acting with autonomy and freedom to develop different solutions to similar problems. Having a common way of working ensures that everybody understands the performance parameters and focuses on delivering results as opposed to solutions.

3   It ensures a common way of measuring people's skills and capabilities

The ability to develop individuals should not include relearning standard ways of working, dependent on the geographical or team environment in which they find themselves. I am currently engaged in coaching a high-performing and inherently talented individual of high potential within one of our customers. He faces significant inter-cultural challenges. If the business were to overlay alternative ways of working, that individual would quickly move from being talented and motivated to being confused and frustrated.

4   It ensures that global customers recognise a common way of working locally

The continued emergence of globally dominant customers has led to the creation of global customer managers within organisations that supply these global customers. It is common for customers to have central buyers who not only purchase products for a number of outlets, but are also charged with agreeing specific activities to support brands at the point of purchase. Having similar ways of working supplemented by local cultural interpretation ensures that the relationships from global customer managers to local sales teams are transparent and connected to similar objectives. Customers would not readily recognise this but they would certainly point out the frailties of the business if this were not the case.

5 Most importantly, it allows businesses to foster a culture where there are opportunities for every employee to maximise their potential within the business

Individuals need to know that there are opportunities for them to build the skills that will equip them to realise their personal ambitions. A brief reflection on our personal experiences as customers and consumers reveals that the world is ever evolving and forcing us to enhance constantly our personal capabilities. Take a look at the world of music. During the course of my generation we have moved from cleaning vinyl records with a soft cloth to downloading music via the internet. We still listen to music but the way we do it is different. Everything evolves, therefore we need training and coaching to ensure that we can all develop our skills to maximise our potential in a way that is appropriate and relevant.

Inspiring the sales organisation with the skills, motivation, capability and leadership to create amazing relationships with customers will ensure that, while managing all aspects of cost control, performance is maximised which in turn means that profitability becomes a habit for the business. Transferable skill sets, lower investment, minimisation of corporate memory loss, quicker and lasting change and extending capability has to be good for individuals, teams, customers, consumers and ultimately organisations.

Key learnings	That's interesting

Action plan	
What could I do?	
Who would it involve?	
When should I aim to have it done by?	
What resources or dependencies are involved?	

Part II

How to release the talents of the sales force

THE CAPABILITIES NECESSARY TO SELL EXCEPTIONAL BRANDS

'If the rate of change on the outside exceeds the rate of change on the inside then the end is near.'

JACK WELCH, former chairman and CEO General Electric Group uccessful sales-based organisations generally have excellent salespeople. Excellence does not come to a business; it has to develop it through clear strategies and a commitment to ensuring that every single person who influences the sale of products to customers has an outstanding knowledge of the required operational standards. These standards, when consistently applied, engage existing and potential customers around the products the organisation provides. At the core of turning your sales force into profit heroes is a clearly defined and measurable set of operating standards through which team leaders can measure and develop individuals.

In this chapter we will:

- discover the distinction between sales teams and key account teams;
- examine a set of good practice account management operating standards;
- look at how you assess and measure operating standards for varying roles within a sales-based organisation; and
- determine the areas of behaviour that influence a team's ability to sell.

Understand the difference between sales teams and key account teams

Outlet segmentation, the grouping of outlets with defined similarities, determines the most suitable product portfolio and brand activities for a business to target. Generally it also defines the frequency and type of sales calls the sales team provides to various customers. Sales management can determine the appropriate type of call for individual outlets within a segment on the following factors.

- A customer's size.
- Whether they are part of a broader retail group or chain.
- Whether they sell significantly more of your products in comparison with other outlets having similar physical or demographic attributes.

- Whether they have the potential to sell significantly more of your products.

More commonly today, companies base segmentation on the consumers' or shoppers' motivations within an outlet. The classification of an outlet determines the optimum type of call that a salesperson should make.

From 2007 onwards we have been retained by an organisation with a retail sales team of some 185 people. They call on a complete spectrum of retail outlets, from small independent convenience stores through to the biggest retailer's largest outlets. The team collectively calls on more than 28,500 outlets in every corner of the United Kingdom. They have a very clear vision of what success looks like: 'Delivering High Performance through the Excellence of Our People'.

They segment their customers into four tiers:

- Hero customers – approximately 2,500 outlets;
- Key customers – approximately 2,200 outlets;
- Supporting customers – approximately 23,200 outlets; and
- Neutral customers – approximately 800 outlets.

The definition of customer segments is very different in every organisation. In this example, Hero customers are part of a significant retail chain that generally generates significantly above average sales volume. A Neutral customer, being at the opposite side of the spectrum, is likely to be a local convenience outlet generating below average sales.

The objectives of a sales call are different for outlets of varying sizes. In a smaller outlet the focus is commonly on nurturing a relationship with a key contact, driving distribution of new products or stock keeping units and ensuring there is an appropriate level of activation of product. Activation means those activities that can encourage consumers or shoppers to purchase your products ahead of your competitors.

In larger outlets that could be part of a larger chain, relationships with the retailer are at two levels. The primary relationship will be in the retailer's head office, commonly with a buying manager. Salespeople support that relationship by creating relationships in stores with the appropriate person – store general manager, head of customer services, sector managers and so on.

This quick examination of varying styles of outlets shows that there are clearly differing skills, knowledge and behaviours that salespeople need to exhibit depending on the dynamics of the customer they are visiting. The skills required of sales teams evolve around the needs of a given customer segment.

I remember being taught how to do the high jump at school. Like everything within our world, things change over time and you have to adapt to stay ahead of your competitors. In the early 1900s the most common method of doing the high jump was the 'Scissors'. Over the course of the following twenty years, athletes became ever more adept at this method and continued to jump higher. The bar had then to be raised in the early 1920s on the introduction of the 'Western Roll'. Athletes made more progress in the 1950s when the 'Straddle' became common practice, and with the introduction of the 'Fosbury Flop' in the late 1960s, competitors were jumping thirty to forty per cent higher than they were in the early 1900s. Just as athletes run faster and jump higher nowadays, so customers demand more in their relationships with suppliers. Sales teams need to work at differing levels and on differing activities depending on the needs of their customers.

We expect salespeople to be multi-talented. They must be able to recognise opportunities in the market. They need to build profitable agreements that are mutually beneficial for both customers and the business they are representing, and to build long-term trust and commitment with their customers. To be able, therefore, to execute the strategy of their business, salespeople need a broad skill set. They have to develop their knowledge, skills and behaviour to build up the right sales competencies. We can call this doing the right things in the right place at the right time.

The main difference between sales teams and key account teams is the way they influence their customers. Each requires different knowledge and skills; in key accounts they need the skills to influence an organisation, while sales teams focus on decision-making individuals.

For a sales team we bring this to life in front of customers through a structured call process supported with selling tools. There are many variants to both a structured call and the selling tools. Working with a broad range of customers has allowed us to see many examples of structured calls, from an 8×6 (eight steps and six tools) to a 6×6, and many other permutations.

Here are a couple of examples of structured call and selling tools:

Example 1

Steps of a call
1   Plan and prepare
2   Approach and check
3   Sales presentation
4   Close the order
5   Take action
6   Record and evaluate

Selling tools
1 Samples
2 Hand-held computer
3 Sales presenter
4 Commercial proposition
5 Customer records
6 Pen

Example 2

Steps of a call
1 Plan and prepare
2 Sales area check
3 Review of objectives
4 Persuasive selling
5 Close
6 Sales activity activation
7 Administration
8 Evaluation

Selling tools
1 Pen
2 Appointment planning slip
3 Sales presenter
4 Business conversation
5 Sample/point of sale
6 Record card

Neither of these, or any other approach, is right or wrong. Like anything else in business, managers base the solution on the optimum performance standards required to meet the relevant selling objectives within the defined customer base.

Skilfully applying knowledge is clearly not enough – it is crucial to define and then embed the core skills of the sales team. We will examine this in the next chapter.

Like salespeople, key account team members need to be familiar with and capable of applying a structured interface with their customers, but this takes the form of an appointment as opposed to a sales call. During an appointment there is greater emphasis on business development/review. Commonly, appointments are not conducted within a store environment. This requires differing skills from a sales call. An example of the steps of a structured appointment is:

1   Preparation and planning
2   Introduction and purpose
3   Agenda outline
4   Business performance review
5   Business proposal (persuasive selling)
6   Closing the deal
7   Administration
8   Evaluation

The customer that we looked at when reviewing outlet segmentation differentiates between members of the sales force and key account managers. Not only through the titles, rewards and recognition that the different team members receive, but also through the skills, knowledge and behaviour that they need within the role.

Later in Part II we will look at the foundation skills of selling that are common to all members of a sales team, from the sales director to the least experienced members of the sales team.

Identify key account management operating standards

*'If the root is not straight the seedling will be crooked.
As the twig is bent so grows the tree.'*

Chinese proverb

Clearly defined operating standards, coupled with motivated and skilled line managers who take accountability and responsibility for the development of their teams by applying engaging learning, will not on their own turn your sales force into profit heroes. Any organisation also has to have outstanding products supported by excellent propositions for their customers and consumers. Coupled together, this is what will deliver an increased customer and consumer commitment to any business.

Our customers often ask us to assess the capability of a sales organisation. They do this for varying reasons.

- 'We have conducted a huge amount of training with our sales teams but we are not sure how effectively it is coming to life on a day-to-day basis.'
- 'We have acquired a new business and we need to create a common approach to selling.'
- 'We are reviewing the frequency we call on our outlet base and the optimum type of sales call needed across the varying types of accounts. We think we may need differing skills for the sales team.'
- 'Due to the diversity of our business in terms of portfolio of products, cultural differences and language we are limited in our ability to plan effectively for succession within our senior sales leadership team.'
- 'Our competitors have increased the size of their sales teams and we need to ensure that we are doing the right things to protect our business.'

Assessment of these questions always requires an understanding of the optimum skill levels required by the relevant sales teams. To do this we have, based on examining lots of varied sales models, defined what we believe is a good practice set of account management operating standards.

We have already recognised that there are different operating standards required by a sales team and a key account team. This is true again if you manage your business through third party sales teams. Within our business, REL, as well as Sales Consulting we also have a Field Marketing Division. Within this division we not only support retailers and suppliers in activating in-store activities like sampling or displays but we also manage sales teams for suppliers. This is how a third party sales team is defined.

We group our good practice standards into six key capability areas:

1   sales strategy;
2   channel strategy;
3   customer business planning;
4   managing customer relationships;
5   point of purchase execution; and
6   measurement of performance.

We then further segment each of these capability areas with clearly defined operating standards. Every person will not require all of these operating standards. The individual's role in representing the business with customers determines the ones that are relevant.

To measure your organisation's progress in implementing good practice, go through the following checklists and tick the appropriate column for your organisation using a simple traffic light formula – Red, we have a problem in this area that needs work now; Amber, we have made progress but there are still things to be done; and Green, we are up to speed in this area. Then consolidate those opinions to form an action plan for the way forward.

1   Sales strategy

Sales annual operating plan

	R	A	G
Strategic sales priorities and targets are set out in the annual operating plan for the year ahead.			
The annual operating plan is aligned to the strategic plans for the business (3–5 years in outlook).			
The annual operating plan has been agreed across the buiness so all functions are aligned to the part they play in its delivery.			

Commercial policy

	R	A	G
A clearly defined commercial policy is in place providing the operating framework by trade channel. The policy outlines pricing and business terms parameters, guidelines on promotional spend and return on investment. It also sets out key business management standards.			
There is a published price list for all products.			
An open, transparent and defensible pricing and terms structure is in place between channels and customers. The business and its customers have based discounts upon agreed conditions resulting in win–win.			
Planned investment with customers is aligned with channel and customer attractiveness and is in line with budgeted levels.			

Market and category assessment

	R	A	G
The sales, marketing and finance teams have jointly undertaken a market review/opportunity analysis highlighting the category, segment/retail format and brand and channel opportunities for the year ahead.			
A cross-functional team has undertaken a thorough competitor assessment for each category, identifying opportunities and threats. These are captured and reflected in the annual operating plan.			
The business has a clearly defined category strategy for developing its brand portfolio in each of the channels in which it is present.			

Channel prioritisation

	R	A	G
The business has assessed the coverage by distributors of the strategic sales channels and made a decision on the route to market that reflects these strengths.			
The sales and marketing teams, with the support of the finance team, have jointly undertaken a channel classification. This identifies which channels are key to the business in terms of weight of business, and which are seen as the strategic growth channels for the future that might warrant a disproportionate level of investment and support now.			

Organisation and capability

	R	A	G
The sales organisation is structured and equipped to achieve the strategic sales priorities.			
A plan to build capability is in place to support the achievement of the sales strategy.			

2   Channel strategy

Channel assessment

	R	A	G
A channel opportunity assessment has identified the macro business opportunities by channel, and channel investment is weighted accordingly.			
A top-level channel 'size of the prize', or business opportunity assessment, has been calculated based upon moving certain key performance indicators in the year ahead, e.g. closing distribution gaps.			
Sub-channels are defined within each channel with clear channel boundaries.			
A route to market assessment has identified the current way of servicing the business and any changes to be made in the year ahead.			
Distributors have been selected by channel according to their ability to service each channel and deliver the required performance for the business's brands.			
A process of ongoing distributor assessment is in place taking account of changes in the market and competitive landscape.			

Channel strategy

	R	A	G
A channel strategy is in place for each major trade channel, detailing the channel objectives, strategic sales priorities and channel volume. There are set revenue targets for the year ahead and these have been translated into an actionable channel plan.			
Business performance targets are set at the channel and sub-channel levels with key sales builder initiatives identified and a channel execution plan.			
The channel planning process takes account of customer goals.			
The KAM (key account manager) is able to explain the channel plan and strategic sales priorities for the year ahead.			
A distributor development plan is in place setting out how the distributor will grow the business over an agreed timescale (3–5 years).			
A contract is in place with each distributor with clear timescales, geographic boundaries and required performance standards.			

Customer prioritisation

	R	A	G
Customers have been prioritised for resource allocation, and the planned investment with customers is based upon an evaluation of past performance, profitability, strategic importance to the business and forecast growth rates for the year ahead.			
The business has reallocated investment with customers based on a robust evaluation of past business activities.			

Organisation

	R	A	G
The structure of account management reflects the sub-channel structure in each channel of business.			
The structure reflects the relative level of influence at head office and outlet level for each sub-channel/account with field resources allocated accordingly.			
The channel resource plan highlights the number of outlets that can be covered in each sub-channel and the field budgets are allocated according to the accounts profitability to the business. These have been given to the account teams to manage.			

	R	A	G
Top customers are distinguished from the less important ones by having a dedicated, more experienced and higher calibre KAM responsible for managing the business.			
The profile of account managers matches the profile of the account, the type of buyers that they are dealing with and the stage of development of business with the customer.			
Junior members of the sales team handle a number of smaller accounts.			

3 Customer business planning

Customer profile and strategy

	R	A	G
The KAM is able to explain the customer's mission statement and overall business strategy in the market.			
The KAM can outline the customer strategy for the relevant categories within which the business operates and knows the importance of the business's brands for the customer.			
The KAM has documented the customer outlet profile by trading format, selling space and fascia.			
The KAM keeps records of trends and customer developments. They identify the impact of these on the business and the action that needs to be taken.			
The KAM can outline likely developments in the customer's business for the next year.			
The KAM is able to translate market trends and customer developments into business growth opportunities for the business.			
The KAM understands the international footprint of the customer's business and their international strategy.			
The KAM understands the strategy of the distributor and the role that their company's brands play in their business and portfolio of products.			
The KAM understands the operation of the distributor's business and how they should influence them to get the best results.			

Consumer and shopper insights

	R	A	G
The KAM has knowledge of shopper/consumer profile by outlet type/fascia for their customer.			
Together with major customer's market research into shopper/consumer, behaviour by outlet profile/fascia has been undertaken.			
The KAM understands consumer trends and how they will affect business with their customer(s).			
There is a defined purchase decision hierarchy by segment/retail format for each trade channel. The consumer motivations that are widely used in the business and applied with customers are understood.			
Joint shopper/consumer research projects have been initiated and have been undertaken with major customers.			
The customer looks to the business as a category adviser whenever trying to build understanding of shoppers/consumers or to gain category insights.			
The customer shares sales and consumer/shopper data with the business, as the business consistently demonstrates the capability to turn such data into insights.			

Category strategy

	R	A	G
A clear category strategy is in place for all major customers defining the key initiatives that will be delivered within the annual plan.			

Outlet mapping

	R	A	G
Following an outlet classification process, outlets have been segmented by type and prioritised according to the size of the opportunity that they represent for the brands or the strategic importance of the outlet.			
Brand execution priorities have been defined by outlet type and these have been translated into monthly field activity plans.			
Outlet information is stored on an outlet database, which is kept updated to reflect new openings and closures. Sales information by outlet is stored on the database.			
The outlet database is used to plan outlet coverage and journey planning for the field sales force.			

Annual account planning

	R	A	G
A jointly written business plan is in place with major customers, reflecting the customer's annual category priorities and the business's strategic sales initiatives.			
There is an opportunity analysis against each of the key sales builders and a 'size of the prize' has been calculated from both the business and the customer's perspective.			
The annual customer business plan has clearly defined objectives that are agreed with the customer and has an agreed means and frequency of measurement.			
The annual customer business plan includes a customer profile, key contacts map defining who makes decisions on what within the customer's business. It has a sales builder plan (including a detailed promotional plan), business terms summary and a volume and revenue forecast to achieve the annual target and objectives.			
The sales builder plan is based on a documented evaluation of past outlet initiatives. Investment is focused on the most effective activities as well as on those new initiatives with the biggest potential business impact.			
Barriers to execution of the sales builder plan have been considered and implementation plans have been adjusted accordingly.			
The business works jointly with the distributor to develop the annual account plans for key customers to ensure that all parties will achieve their business objectives.			

Activity/sales builder planning

	R	A	G
KAMs are presented with a commercial calendar a year in advance, detailing the key initiatives for the year ahead in order to enable effective annual planning with the customer.			
A customer planning process is in place whereby the details of each brand initiative are confirmed, and selling tools provided, for KAMs to sell in brand initiatives according to the lead times of each customer.			
The sales builder calendar reflects the customer themes and includes tailor-made activities that provide the customer with a point of difference in the market place.			
The KAM is responsible for forecasting the business on a minimum of a 12-week rolling cycle, particularly in respect of volume. This forecast drives initiatives that are planned with the customer and will affect the normal rate of sale.			
An evaluation of customer investment process is in place whereby KAMs evaluate the cost and revenue impact of proposed activities prior to formulating business proposals for customers. The evaluation includes the value created for the business, value for the customer and the effect on the overall relevant category or segment/retail format.			
Non-productive investment with customers has been reallocated to more effective sales builder activities.			
All sales builder activities have pre-determined objectives.			
Minimum operating targets are agreed with the distributor against key brand initiatives/customer activities.			

Leveraging resources

	R	A	G
Resource is focused according to channel and customer priorities.			
The organisation structure reflects the customer's organisational structure as much as possible.			
The KAM involves other functions in the business planning process.			
The KAM secures support from marketing for implementation of brand initiatives for his/her customer.			

4 Managing customer relationships

Selling and negotiation

	R	A	G
The KAM follows a structured selling approach for each proposal that is taken to the customer. It includes effective questioning techniques to uncover customer needs.			
The KAM is capable of overcoming customer objections and consistently gains advantage over the competition through superior business proposals and strong persuasive selling skills.			
All KAMs demonstrate effective negotiation techniques and application of principles by, for example, enforcing the conditions of trade terms.			
All KAMs plan terms negotiations thoroughly in advance, producing a negotiating strategy with clearly defined positions, wish list and tradable concessions identified.			
All KAMs look for a win–win outcome from negotiations, recognising the importance of maintaining the ongoing business relationship.			

Business proposals

	R	A	G
Business proposals reflect the strategic sales priorities of the business translated into customer-specific plans.			
Business proposals are submitted on time, in the format/language preferred by the customer and to the required standard.			
Business proposals are based on consumer/shopper insights drawn from the customer's business and with a clearly quantified business benefit to the customer.			
Business proposals reflect robust evaluation of past activities, so the activities that work for the business and for the customer are those that are proposed again.			
The KAM will propose tailor-made activities to the customer that give them a competitive point of difference in the market place.			
Category proposals add value to the category and are tailored to meet category objectives.			
Business proposals deliver an acceptable level of profitability to the category.			
The KAM ensures that their customer is first to market with innovation, by taking concepts to the customer early and gaining internal agreement to grant the customer exclusivity for a limited period.			
The KAM is able to build compelling internal business proposals to influence senior managers within the business.			
Sales and finance sign off all terms proposals internally before the KAM takes them to a customer.			

Decision mapping

	R	A	G
The KAM has mapped out the decision-making process within the customer's business and knows the key people involved.			
The KAM understands the customer decision-making process for different types of proposal, e.g. promotions, range changes, equipment placement in outlet and so on. They know who the decision-makers are, and what the stage gates are that each proposal must pass through.			
The KAM is able to navigate and effectively influence the customer organisation in order to gain agreement to a proposed course of action.			
The KAM can make decisions, without defaulting to higher authority.			

Meeting management

	R	A	G
The KAM conducts at least monthly business reviews at which they review performance against targets set in the annual plan, implementation of agreed activities and identify where corrective action should be taken.			
Monthly business reviews follow a structured approach with the customer that reflects company standards and training received.			
Competitive consumer pricing in the market is a regular agenda item in business review meetings.			

Contact management

	R	A	G
The KAM has a contact strategy for all the key people within the customer's organisation (vertical and horizontal). They match them with the corresponding person in their organisation, detailing clear objectives for each contact. They define the frequency of, and means of contact (formal/social) and an agreed agenda/brief.			
Top-level discussions between the senior management of the local organisation (minimum sales director level) and the customer's organisation (minimum buying director level) take place at least once a year to review performance and agree future strategic business priorities.			
Functional specialists within the business have direct contact with their counterparts in the customer organisation and the KAM is kept informed of the outcome of all contacts.			
Top-level discussions are held at a minimum frequency of once a year when the senior management of the business meets with the senior management of the distributor to review performance and agree future strategic priorities.			

Managing customer business teams

	R	A	G
The KAM leverages cross-functional resources, e.g. logistics and marketing, in order to deliver the optimal results for their customer.			
The KAM leads a cross-functional team of specialists assigned to supporting the development of the customer's business.			
Effective customer and consumer marketing support is in place to support KAMs working with major customers.			
Members of the marketing function are assigned to support the KAM in demonstrating a detailed knowledge of the customer's promotional and merchandising strategy, and has direct contact with their counterparts in the customer's organisation.			
The KAM manages and motivates key account executives and other support staff directly allocated to the account. They are responsible for their personal development and career progression. They are their team's line manager, coach and mentor.			
Clear lines of responsibility exist between the key roles working on an account.			
The KAM is able to lead and manage collaborative working programmes with the customer ensuring that ownership is taken on both sides for the implementation of initiatives.			
The KAM is able to identify strategic business opportunities and is able to convert these into tangible action plans working with the customer.			
Distributor agreements actively discourage distributors from operating outside of their contractually agreed geographical boundaries.			

Service

	R	A	G
The KAM has an agreed frequency of contact with their buyer both face-to-face and by phone or e-mail.			
The KAM monitors service levels to the customer and reviews service issues internally, pre-empting customer notification.			
The KAM handles issues and requests efficiently and promptly.			

Skills and capability

	R	A	G
A suite of relevant functional training programmes is in place to ensure that KAMs have the required commercial skills to manage and develop the business with major customers.			
KAMs have a breadth of commercial experience gained in different parts of the business and in other organisations.			
The KAM consistently demonstrates the core competencies for managing major customers, including strategic thinking, drive for results, persuasive skills and leadership.			
Each KAM has a development plan tailored to their individual needs that addresses personal development areas, management competencies and functional skills.			

5 Point of purchase (POP) execution

Format strategy

	R	A	G
The business has a defined POP vision by channel and outlet type based upon extensive consumer/shopper research.			
There is a defined strategy by channel, customer and format for delivering the POP vision.			
There is a clear commercial rationale for how products should be merchandised in outlet.			
The business delivers POP initiatives that are jointly developed with the customer and tailored by format.			

Sales builder execution

	R	A	G
The business achieves greater presence at the POP than their market share would suggest.			
Sales builder initiatives have a high impact in outlet.			
Sales builder initiatives are easy to execute in outlet, reflecting a good level of operational insight.			
Pricing data on the business and competitor brands is captured from a representative panel of outlets for each customer on a weekly basis, and fed back to the KAM at the start of each week.			
Execution of sales builder activity is reviewed with the customer as part of the monthly business. Corrective steps, when required, are agreed.			
Availability is a key sales force focus and issues that cannot be resolved at an outlet level are fed back to the KAM on a weekly basis.			
Effective merchandising, display and point of sale material support POP activities.			
The KAM makes outlet visits before every customer meeting and records observations on a standard outlet audit form. This is copied to the salesperson responsible for each outlet with comments and customer feedback.			
The business conducts audits of outlets serviced by the distributor and gives feedback on the level of execution being achieved – whether it exceeds, meets or is below expectations.			

Field resource

	R	A	G
A field sales force is in place (either in-house or third party) to build the business's presence in outlet by delivering improvements on all sales builders.			
The field sales force goes through structured sales training to equip them with the skills to fulfil their role in calling, including setting call objectives, following the steps of the call, overcoming customer objections and gaining agreement.			
The field sales force is well equipped with 'tools of trade' in order to be effective in calls (merchandise, display materials, point of sale materials and so on).			
The field sales force follows a defined series of steps in a call and accurately records a summary of every call made.			
The field sales force uses a standardised outlet audit form or hand-held palmtop to record outlet data in calls.			

	R	A	G
The field sales force tracks the business's and competitors' assortment, pricing, share of shelf space, promotional and display activity.			
Call outcomes are transmitted and consolidated electronically and held within an easily accessed central database.			
The KAM harnesses all available resources to achieve high levels of in-outlet execution.			
The distributor sales force primarily gives focus to the businesses' brands during a call.			

Coverage

	R	A	G
The KAM is responsible for defining the coverage strategy for their customers' outlets, subject to agreed resourcing levels and budgets.			
The coverage strategy details the role in call, frequency of visit and approach by format- and customer-specific procedures.			
A detailed and accurate outlet database exists that generates territory maps. The KAM is responsible for ensuring that the outlet data is kept up to date with new outlet openings.			
The field sales force visits all outlets on an agreed frequency.			
The cost and effectiveness of field activity is assessed on the minimum of a yearly basis.			
Resources are redistributed to reflect changes in the trading environment, customers and channel developments.			
There is a process or tool in place that minimises travel time between calls thereby maximising time in call.			
The distributor has a clear coverage plan for their customer's outlets.			

Communication of priorities

	R	A	G
The KAM is responsible for setting outlet objectives at a channel level.			
KAMs brief the field sales force on outlet objectives and outlet priorities for the following periods on a monthly frequency as a minimum.			
The field sales force are notified a month in advance of new priorities so that they can give outlet staff notice in advance of the start date of an activity.			

6   *Measurement of performance*

Scorecard

	R	A	G
The KAM and customer jointly track monthly business performance using a standard scorecard with an agreed set of measures.			
The scorecard is accepted as the common measurement tool for measuring business performance. It reflects customer and the business's key performance indicators. Performance against key performance indicators are formally reviewed once a month as a minimum.			
The business has agreed a set of performance measures with the distributors, tracked on a monthly basis.			
Distributor performance is monitored through monthly sales reporting and random outlet checks, specifically focusing on international customers. Corrective steps are put in place where there is a shortfall against planned performance or where agreed levels of execution are not being achieved.			

Customer investment evaluation

	R	A	G
Year-to-date customer investment (trade spend) is reviewed against budget at the minimum of once a month.			
A process for monitoring trade spends is in place and owned by the finance department.			
Finance managers formally review trade spend with KAMs at the minimum on a monthly basis.			
Sales builder activity post-implementation is evaluated against pre-defined objectives to identify effectiveness of different mechanics and payback against forecast levels.			
The effectiveness of overall trade spend by customer is evaluated, including terms, once a year as a minimum.			

Customer feedback

	R	A	G
An independent audit of customer satisfaction and business attitude is conducted once a year in order to assess the business's relationship with major customers.			
Major customers are asked to give feedback as part of an individual KAM's development plan, including participating in 360° surveys.			

Customer profit and loss(P&L) account

	R	A	G
Customer P&Ls are in place for all major accounts to a customer contribution, or net profit level, with fully allocated sales overheads.			
The KAM has a working knowledge of the customer P&L.			
The finance team manage customer P&Ls and review them at least once a month with the KAM and sales director when necessary.			
Target levels of profitability by customer are set as part of the annual operating planning process, reflecting forecast volume and revenue and budgeted investment levels.			
Sales costs are tracked as percentage of total revenue.			

Personal performance

	R	A	G
KAMs are measured on sales volume, gross and net revenue and customer profitability.			
Line managers measure KAM's personal performance against annual targets and development areas twice a year as a minimum.			

Summary – populating the template on the next page to identify your areas of opportunity

Key to addressing opportunities is identifying your strengths to leverage. Having added up your areas of strength by adding up the number you have marked as green, find out where to concentrate your effort on improving your sales practices: count up the red and amber indicators in each area, and calculate what percentage are red or amber. This will identify in which areas of best practice your biggest opportunities may be.

Area of best practice	Red	Amber	Green	No. of items	% red	% amber	% green
1 Sales strategy				14			
2 Channel strategy				20			
3 Customer business planning				40			
4 Managing customer relationships				42			
5 Point of purchase execution				33			
6 Measurement of performance				18			

As we move into Chapter 5, we will examine how to make progress on the core skills of the sales team, which is the vital foundation for developing the broader sales operational capabilities of your organisation.

Assess and measure operating standards for varying roles within a sales-based organisation

'... *Difficult times lie ahead. Soon we must all face the choice between what is right and what is easy.*'

J.K. ROWLING, author
(Professor Dumbledore: *The Goblet of Fire*)

To assess operating standards there are a number of elements for you to consider, including the following.

- Establishing what the appropriate level of skill for each of the operating standards is, dependent on the role of the individual within the sales function.

- Giving customers formal opportunities to contribute to, and influence the company's strategy, skills development priorities and ways of working. This then allows the business to align solutions more closely to the needs of the customers – the impact of that, is improved customer loyalty.
- For the salespeople themselves it provides clear priorities for their personal development, while determining the skills and knowledge they need to develop in order to further their career within sales.

It is common to task human resources to develop an annual performance review that includes the assessment of levels of skill and critically, behaviour. It is, however, the responsibility of the sales arm of the business to determine the level of functional skill required for any given role.

Having determined the appropriate operational standards required for any role within the sales function you need to determine the level of application required for each of these standards.

Following the establishment of the good practice set of operating standards, our attention turns to the assessment of these specific capabilities. For us, simplicity is important. To provide simplicity of assessment against these standards we recommend a three-tier measurement process.

- Does the individual *beat* the required standard?
- Does the individual *meet* the required standard?
- Is the individual *below* the required standard?

The standard requirement will vary depending on the medium to long-term goals of the organisation. In looking at a couple of operational standards we can see how we can construct meaningful measurements of performance.

Example 1

Managing customer relationships – skills and capability

A suite of relevant functional training programmes is in place to ensure that KAMs have the required commercial skills to manage and develop the business with major customers.
KAMs have a breadth of commercial experience gained in different parts of the business and experience gained in other organisations.
The KAM consistently demonstrates the core competencies for managing major customers, including strategic thinking, drive for results, persuasive skills and leadership.
Each KAM has a development plan tailored to their individual needs that addresses personal development areas, management competencies and functional skills.

Overall rating:		
Below:	Meets:	Beats:
The KAM is an experienced salesperson but may lack formal training.	The KAM has a breadth of commercial experience and has taken part in structured training in managing major customers.	The KAM demonstrates the core competencies for their role and a breadth of commercial expertise and functional skills gained from relevant training programmes. KAM has an orientation towards continued self-improvement through their personal development plan.

Example 2

Sales strategy – sales annual operating plan

Strategic sales priorities and targets are set out in the annual operating plan that has been agreed for the year ahead.		
The annual operating plan is aligned to the strategic plans for the business (3–5 years in outlook).		
The annual operating plan has been agreed across the business so all functions are aligned to the part that they play in its delivery.		
Overall rating:		
Below:	Meets:	Beats:
Sales targets exist for the year ahead but no strategic sales priorities have been communicated in the business.	Sales targets and strategic sales priorities have been communicated throughout the sales organisation.	Sales targets and strategic sales priorities have been communicated throughout the sales organisation and across other functions.

Once you have defined the standards for each skill level and the operational skill level for each role, you can assess the sales team members against them. Support this further with an assessment of the appropriate level of behaviour to determine the priority development areas of the team member.

Consolidating the assessment across the entire sales function then defines the priority areas of team development. Once embedded through our recommended approach to achieve maximum engagement, retention and recall, and reinforced through consistent on the job coaching from line managers, you are well on your way to 'Turning your sales force into profit heroes'.

The impact of behaviour

> *'I admire his work, but I couldn't warm to him if I was cremated next to him.'*
> **KEITH RICHARDS, guitarist and songwriter**

It is straightforward to identify both skills and behaviours. These will change given the relevant business dynamics and cultural influences.

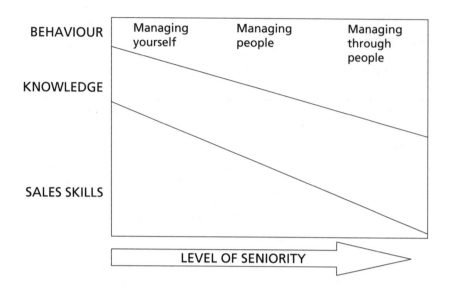

With one of our customers we explored the above model. It suggests that capability development in respect of behaviours become more important the more senior the role an individual holds within a team or organisation.

When 'managing yourself', team working, for example, is of vital relevance. When 'managing people' you need to supplement your behavioural skills with coaching and training capability, project management, performance management and decision making. While at the most senior levels, where individuals are 'managing through people', individuals need to excel at change management, delegation, influencing, crisis management and emotional intelligence.

Skills and knowledge alone will not unlock your team's inner strength. You have to make sure that individuals are coached and trained in building their behavioural capability. Only then will the investment in developing skills and knowledge be effectively brought to life for your customers.

Key learnings	That's interesting

Action plan	
What could I do?	
Who would it involve?	
When should I aim to have it done by?	
What resources or dependencies are involved?	

5

THE SKILLS TO SELL
EXCEPTIONAL BRANDS

'If Thomas Edison had gone to business school, we would all be reading by bigger candles.'

MARK McCORMACK, *author*

Having defined the operational standards required of the varying roles within your sales team, you will be in a position to equip every member of the sales force with foundation skills. If you look up the dictionary definition of the word 'foundation' you find: 'the basic experience, idea or attitude on which a way of life or belief is based' or 'a construction below the ground that distributes the load of a building, wall etc.'. Foundation sales skills are relevant for any person within an organisation who has some responsibility for selling. In its simplest form I, like many others, describe selling as 'helping people to buy things'.

You can have superb brands with a unique attraction for your target consumers, but unless you target retail outlets and distribute the brands in the correct formats/pack types they will always remain out of reach of consumers. Determining the right outlets, pricing, route to market are all critically important, but without a salesperson who can effectively work with existing and potential customers the product, on any given metric, will not be a success. Equipping the sales team with, and measuring them against the foundation skills relevant to your organisational and customers' needs, ensures that the sales team firmly establishes any brand or product at the point of purchase.

In this chapter we will:

- define the core skills of an effective sales team; and
- define the components of the individual foundation skills areas.

The core skills of an effective sales team

'If you really want something in this life, you have to work for it. Now quiet! They're about to announce the lottery numbers ...'

HOMER SIMPSON

Every one of our clients recognises that they have to build the skills of both individuals and teams in order to outperform their competitors and grow market share. Very few businesses have the luxury of their customers routinely purchasing their services without any need for the supplier to sell the offering to them. Yes, there are commodities that are, at a given point in time, unique with a high level of consumer demand and awareness. However, competitors soon emerge, putting pressure on the supplier to differentiate their offer to maintain the customer commitment.

In 2007 I purchased a new car. I spent quite some time looking at what I would like to buy. With a young family I considered such aspects as safety and practicality, while also having a keen eye on what was suitable for business purposes. Not least of all the criteria, it had to be a vehicle that I would enjoy on a day-to-day basis. Having decided on and ordered my car, I had a twelve-week wait in eager anticipation of receiving my new vehicle. Having chosen the car and accessories, I then had to organise the various aspects associated with being legally compliant. One such aspect is car insurance. Given the vehicle I was buying, my choices were extremely limited. My existing insurers wanted me to have additional elements of security factory-fitted to the vehicle, and the story was similar with nearly all insurers I asked to quote. I returned to the car dealership and explained the predicament. They said that they had one provider who would be able to offer me the insurance I required. With the time fast approaching for my car to be delivered I contacted their recommended insurer, and sure enough this company was able to organise the required level of car insurance. The dealership had solved my problem.

A year later came the point of renewing the insurance policy. Like everything today, despite not having had any claims, the renewal notice came with the not unforeseen uplift in premiums. I decided to once again 'shop around' to find alternatives with the ultimate aim of securing the same level of insurance at a cheaper cost.

Once again I spoke with a variety of companies, did an online comparison, and found what on face value looked like a really competitive option. I spoke with the potential provider and they were excellent. They listened to my needs and got a real grasp for my current situation. In turn they came back to me with options and agreed to outperform any competitive quote. Sometimes in life it is easier to maintain the status quo so I spoke to my existing provider and explained that I had received a quotation thirty-five per cent lower than the renewal premium that they had quoted me. After a period of consideration they came back and offered me the insurance at the same premium their competitor had quoted.

So did the existing provider retain my business? They had eventually offered me the same price as the company that I had contacted. I knew the service they offered. It was the same as they had been providing me with for the previous year. They kept on phoning to ask if I had made a decision. Well, I chose *not* to renew with the existing provider and instead opted for the new insurer. My reasons for doing so were numerous. I found it incredible that they had the audacity to send a renewal quotation that I could so easily improve on. Did they truly believe that I would not look into finding cheaper alternatives? Did they not realise that I could get the same benefits from another provider significantly cheaper? I felt as it they were 'taking me for a ride'. The other insurer listened to my needs and proposed alternatives, packaged in what, I felt, was a caring service.

The lesson is that you can provide the same service at the same price of your competitors but if you do not really listen to the needs of your customers and offer them competitive alternatives that are rooted in their needs, you will not be able to reap the benefits of a trusted relationship between supplier and customer that will grow over time.

There are many varying models for defining the core skills required by a sales team, but they do all have a number of elements in common.

- We have to listen to customers to understand their needs.
- We need to propose solutions and propositions that are based on the needs of the customers and in turn, the consumers.
- We have to listen to objections and overcome or outweigh them.
- We have to provide win–win solutions.
- We need to adapt our style to the style of the customer.
- We have to translate the features of the offering into tangible benefits for the customer and then in turn, the consumer.

Salespeople need all of the core skills if they are to engage customers in an offering. They are not exclusive. As with a jigsaw puzzle you need all the pieces if you are to see the results of your hard work. In other words, if one element is not coached and developed with the sales team, the net result will be that you are not helping the customer to buy from you. So as opposed to looking at these as individual components, we refer to them as a series of modules as they are all integral to each other.

Our good practice set of foundation skills fall into a six-piece jigsaw:

The components of the six areas of foundation skills

Communicating with customers

'There is now a support group for compulsive talkers. It's called On Anon Anon.'
> **PAULA POUNDSTONE, stand-up comic**

This module is about communicating with customers more effectively and efficiently through building rapport, using effective listening and questioning, and adapting one's style and approach to the attitude and interpersonal style of the customer.

This skill area has a structured approach to questioning in order to develop effective conversations with customers. It looks at the keys to good listening and at what can go wrong when you are listening. It looks at verbal and non-verbal buying signals and the importance of body language. Finally, it identifies the different interpersonal styles we all have and how to deal most effectively with them.

We have developed tools to put any given proposition to a customer. The 'Developing the Conversation' template assists salespeople to follow a structured and more effective approach when making customer propositions. The 'Style Identifier' matrix supports this. There are a number of variants of style identifier, and our approach is rooted in the thinking of Osgood and Leary. It helps to identify one of four natural styles of a customer, allowing the salesperson to adapt their own style and behaviour accordingly.

When this foundation skill is embedded within the organisation, salespeople will be consistently able to:

- listen and question more effectively when interacting with customers;
- recognise and identify different personal styles people have, allowing a salesperson to adapt their personal style to that of the customers; and
- develop conversations in a structured way when making proposals to customers.

Listening and questioning
Good listening is the most valuable tool to use in understanding a customer's needs. Active listening is an effective way to encourage people to speak and open up to you, through non-verbal communication and body language. There are a few simple hints and tips to ensure that we do this well.

- Whenever possible, make notes while the customer speaks. This is a very effective way of demonstrating that you are finding the things they say so important that you need to write them down.

- Always smile or show a positive expression when the customer speaks. They will feel more comfortable and speak more freely.
- Always make eye contact. This will establish trust between you and the customer, showing them that you have nothing to hide.
- Don't keep anything crossed. Don't cross your arms or your legs. Crossing your arms means, to the other person, that you are shutting yourself off from them, you are trying to hide something or you are defending yourself.

There are elements that can make your listening ineffective. Here are some examples.

- Jumping to conclusions before the customer finishes their sentence. This can show that you have already decided whether you agree with them or not. Had you waited for them to finish their sentence, you might have found out they were actually saying something very different from what you thought they were going to say.
- Prejudices; your listening can become selective when the customer is talking about something you have a strong opinion about.
- Lack of attention; you can probably think three times faster than the customer can talk. If you don't focus your mind on what they are saying, your thoughts can wander off.
- You talk too much; you have two ears and one mouth, so use them in the same proportion! When you talk the customer can't talk, and that is just broadcasting which makes for ineffective listening.

Research shows that we only communicate 7% of our feelings and attitudes with words, and 38% of our feelings and attitudes by the tone of our voice. Finally, we communicate 55% of our feelings and attitudes through non-verbal expressions.

This means that when you listen, you will gain a better understanding of the customer if you pay close attention to their body language. Are they smiling, are their arms crossed, are they leaning backwards or forwards, are they looking into your eyes when they speak? Listen to the tone of their voice – this will tell you more about what their feelings are than just the words they are using.

With listening comes questioning, which is crucial to making a successful customer proposition. The best way to understand a customer's needs and the way that they make decisions is to use a structured questioning approach, of which there are four primary types:

1   Open questions: usually questions about general topics relevant to the customer and their business.
2   Probing questions: used to get a better understanding of a specific topic, or can be used to guide the conversation in the direction of the point you would eventually like to make.
3   Closed questions: used to get the customer to agree to a specific point, or check facts that you know the customer can confirm.
4   Rhetorical question: that gives the answer to the question as well. All you want the customer to do is to agree with what you are saying at this particular moment.

The four questioning types come together to form the questioning pyramid:

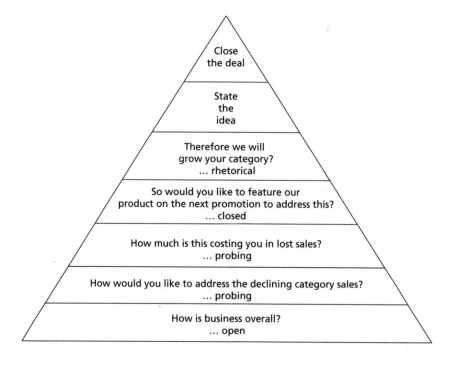

Recognising different personal styles

When people get together they, knowingly or unknowingly, start to collect information in order to form an opinion about what type of person they have in front of them. Everyone has a natural wish to control the situation they are in. It is therefore important to know, for example, whether the other person is more dominating than you, or more people-oriented or task-oriented than you. From this we form our opinion of the natural style of the other person.

Your aim is to recognise whether someone is more push- or pull-oriented, and whether they are more people- or task-oriented. Someone who is more push-oriented is someone who likes to control their environment by being more overtly dominant. A pull-oriented person still wants to be in control, but does this in a way that is more difficult to read – hence a covertly dominant person.

There are no right or wrong natural styles. Someone's interpersonal style is part of their personality, a mix of genetics, upbringing, education, experience and so on. This does not mean that people can only behave in a certain way and have no control over this. We are talking here about the style someone is most comfortable with. Being able to recognise your customer's natural style and adapt your own style accordingly greatly increases the effectiveness and efficiency of communication.

The style indicator tool helps you to identify quickly someone's preferred style allowing you then to adapt your method of communication with them appropriately.

Different interpersonal styles can be grouped into four distinct types; conceptual, social, analytical and direct.

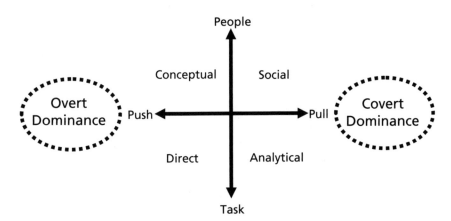

There are key traits of preferences dependent on the preferred style. These preferences then indicate how you should deal with a person with a specific style preference, and what you need to watch out for in any given style, if it is your preference.

Conceptuals

- *May only read summary/recommendations*

If you are dealing with a Conceptual	If you are a Conceptual
Ensure proposals are clear and short Use bullet points 'Capture the imagination' Keep them involved Talk 'big picture'.	Focus on the detail Don't get carried away Keep to the point Ensure that you stick to the matter at hand.

Socials

- *Dislike formality*
- *Are hard to give tough feedback to*

If you are dealing with a Social	If you are a Social
Meet to discuss proposals Listen – if they are raising difficulties they may be trying to let you down gently Make the proposal a dialogue Don't deadline them Keep it relaxed.	Watch out for being too relaxed Have the data Prepare to be pithy Watch the time Be responsive.

Analyticals

- *Will investigate all the relevant detail*
- *Believe that data accuracy is critical*

If you are dealing with an Analytical	If you are an Analytical
Make sure the detail is right Know your stuff Show alternatives considered Don't push Don't expect too much feedback Present formally.	Don't get lost in the detail Keep sight of the bigger picture Thoroughness must not turn into nit-picking Watch your pace.

Directs

- *Tend to need summary and recommendations*
- *Will explore the detail if they think you are flaky*

If you are dealing with a Direct	If you are a Direct
Clear summary and proposals Be logical and data-driven Focus on the bottom line Pacey Present confidently.	Be aware of your ability to intimidate – step back (unless you choose to exploit this situation) Give others time to consider their thoughts Watch out for arrogance.

The style indicator tool is a quick exercise to complete. In order to see how it works I would suggest that you could initially identify your own personal style.

Read the phrases across and for each pair think about which one of the two statements most closely reflects your personal style and mark an x in the bracket beside the appropriate descriptor. For this example I have marked what I believe to be my personal style. There are two scales that you will need to complete.

Scale A

(x) more dominant	( ) or more easy-going
(x) more taking charge	( ) or more go-along
(x) more assertive	( ) or more hesitant
(x) more challenging	( ) or more accepting
( ) more active	(x) or more thoughtful
( ) more confronting	(x) or more supporting
(x) more talkative	( ) or more quiet
(x) more bold	( ) or more retiring
( ) more intense	(x) or more relaxed
(x) more forceful	( ) or more subtle

Now total only the second column, which in my case is 3. You now need to complete the same for scale B

Scale B

(x) more informal	( ) or more formal
( ) more spontaneous	(x) or more disciplined
( ) more impulsive	(x) or more self-controlled
( ) more responsive	(x) or more methodical
(x) more close	( ) or more distant
( ) more feeling	(x) or more thinking
(x) more people-orientated	( ) or more task-orientated
(x) more outgoing	( ) or more reserved
( ) more dramatic	(x) or more matter-of-fact
( ) more warm	(x) or more cool

This time total only the first column, in my case 4.

You will now need to transfer these to the grid on the opposite page to identify your personal style preference: Mark on the x axis your answer for scale A and on the y axis your answer for scale B.

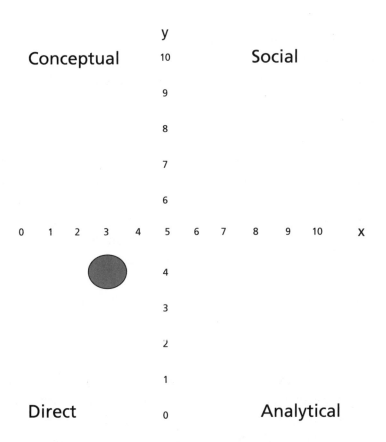

From the example of my personal style preferences we can see that I have a preference for a more direct style yet not overtly so.

By following a similar exercise for yourself and your key customer contacts, you can determine how you need to flex your own style so that you connect more effectively with the style preference of your contact.

Developing conversations in a structured way

Developing a conversation with a customer maximises the likelihood of the customer saying 'yes' to a proposition. The conversation has to be developed step by step: 'State your idea, outline the benefits, and close the deal'. When you get to that point you have to be confident the customer will agree with your proposal. The 'art' of selling is knowing when to move from one phase to the next and go for the close. It is about how to influence the shape and structure of a conversation with customers.

Here's an example of how to develop the conversation.

Situation
You are approaching the year-end, and your brand is underperforming with this customer compared with the mean performance of the category and the channel. Through your store visits you have noticed that the best-selling stock keeping unit (SKU) is under-represented on the shelf, with only 2 facings versus 4 facings in most other stores, and your product can only be found on the bottom shelf. At the same time the customer is selling a competitor's product with a five times smaller market share with 4 facings at eye level on the shelves. The Christmas season is a peak sales period for your product and you have not yet received the customer's display orders.

Building rapport
Even when you are in a hurry and keen to discuss your important issue with your customer, you need to start the conversation slowly and allow a couple of minutes to get used to each other, know what is on the customer's mind today and develop the personal relationship. This conversation can be started by some very simple questions such as: 'did you have a good journey, how was your holiday?' These are usually 'open' questions.

Open questions
Next we direct the conversation towards business by asking general questions to the customer, such as:

- 'How are the category sales doing?'
- 'How is the Christmas build-up?'
- 'What do you expect from Christmas this year?'
- 'When are you starting your Christmas promotions?'

It is important that you broadly cover topics that are relevant to the customer but outside the proposition you would like to make. By taking time, listening to the customer and observing his or her behaviour very carefully, you can pick up a lot of information and signals that are important for the rest of the discussion.

Probing questions

When you believe you have covered most of the areas you wanted to cover through open questions, or when you would like to explore a specific point that has come up while asking open questions, you ask a probing question. In our example we would like to hear the customer's view about what to do about the underperformance of your product in their store: 'You say *your product* sales are not growing as fast as the market average. How can we resolve this?'

Closed questions

After you have established through probing questions that one of the reasons your product is underperforming is a lack of visibility and store promotions, and the customer has indicated they would like to do something extra with your brand you can ask a closed question: 'Would you like to order an extra display of the SKU?'

Rhetorical question

When you have discussed your product proposition and received positive signals from the customer, you could ask a rhetorical question: 'So with a better shelf position and a secondary display we can anticipate a 40% increase in sales?'

State the idea

When the customer agrees with your rhetorical question you can state your proposition: 'You would like to move *the product* to an eye-level shelf and double its facings from 2 to 4. You would also like to order an extra display unit to be placed in the store.'

Outline the benefits

To make it easier for the customer to say 'yes', you summarise what the benefits are for the customer once more: 'Increased sales of a fast-moving item, bringing store performance in line with the market, additional "impulse" sales through an additional display.'

Close the deal

At the end you ask the customer to say 'yes' if they have not already done so.

Overcoming objections

> *'Just as a river has two banks, so every matter has two sides.'*
>
> **Chinese proverb**

This module is about overcoming objections and getting the customer to say 'yes' more frequently. It demonstrates that objections are often questions based on misunderstandings. Objections can be buying signals, and you will have heard most objections before. This module introduces a structured approach to handling objections.

When this foundation skill is embedded within the organisation, salespeople will be able to consistently:

- identify what are the most common objections made by customers;
- recognise when a buyer is applying his or her 'golden rules';
- turn objections into opportunities; and
- use a structured approach to overcome customer objections.

Customers or buyers are trained to make objections; it is their job. It helps them to secure better propositions from their suppliers and therefore creates enhanced profitability for them, possibly at your expense.

When the customer says 'no', stay calm. Try to listen and understand why they are making their objection. It may be because they do not understand what you are proposing. It can also be a buying signal; the customer is interested but needs more convincing that what they are agreeing to is the most appropriate thing for their business.

Objections generally fall into five common areas.

- The product or its quality; for example, buying a new product with a new label when they still have stock of the old label.

- Aspects associated with customer service; for example, they can only order once a week.
- Pricing or payment terms; for example, they have a concern about the margin that they are making on the given product, or an objection to their payment terms or credit limit.
- Insufficient space in outlet to accommodate the proposal.
- Equipment; for example, if the product requires new refrigeration they are concerned not only about the space to accommodate the refrigeration, but also the additional electricity cost.

With common areas of objections it is critical to prepare for them by creating standard arguments to overcome them.

No matter at what level you are dealing with a customer, remember that what is good for you is not automatically good for the customer. By taking the customer's views and opinions into consideration early in the planning of any event or activity it is possible to negate this and make clear what is in it for them. The fact still remains that it is the buyer's duty to negotiate the best possible deal with a salesperson. Buyers in large retail groups are specifically trained in making objections, and behaving in ways that try to undermine the seller's confidence in order to get the best value for their business.

Early in my career I was working as an area manager for a large retail group in the UK specialising in the sale of beverage alcohol. I had the opportunity of spending four months working on secondment within the buying team for the business, and the first thing I was told on the first day was to say 'no' to everything, as there was always a better deal to be had from suppliers.

As a generalisation we can assume that there are ten 'golden rules' that buyers either consciously or sub-consciously think about.

1 Always say 'no' first. If you say 'yes' right away you have given away value to the supplier. You have to assume that they had left room to negotiate their offer.
2 Never show enthusiasm in front of a supplier. If you show enthusiasm, the supplier will take advantage of you and not offer you the best possible deal.

3 Always talk price and margin. No matter how many features and benefits the supplier offers you, only talk about price and margin. Do not give the supplier an opportunity to justify a better price or margin for a specific reason. Tell them you are not interested in what is so special about the product or promotion the supplier is offering – you are only comparing prices with competitive offerings.

4 Consistently ask for the impossible. A supplier's confidence will be undermined when you never seem to be satisfied with whatever offer is put in front of you. In order to 'please you' the supplier's initial offer will already be a good one, because they know what reaction they will get from you.

5 Tell them 'You will have to significantly improve your offer'. Always expect the supplier to have plenty of room to negotiate. Tell them to give all of that up right away.

6 Always be someone's second fiddle. Always make it clear that you report to someone above you who has set you clear goals and objectives. Even if you would personally like the offer, you would still have to answer to someone higher up.

7 Never close a deal without getting something in return. Make it known that you are doing the supplier 'a favour' by accepting their offer, and you expect them to do something extra in return.

8 Play the 'good cop, bad cop'. Work in pairs and confuse the supplier by each behaving very differently. One plays the 'good cop' who is open to reason while the other is completely unreasonable and demands outrageous things from the supplier.

9 Use the salami-slicing tactic – break everything down. Never accept a package deal, judge every component on its own merit and negotiate each item separately.

10 Use the Columbo tactic. After the supplier thinks they have closed the deal and have given everything they are prepared to give, ask for something new or extra. Nine out of ten times they will give it to save the bigger deal.

Handling objections is a foundation skill of salespeople recognised in every major organisation with a sales team. From a broad array of approaches we coach line managers to embed the following approach to overcoming objections in a structured fashion.

K – eep cool and calm
  Keep any sign of anger or frustration out of your response.
L – isten
  Demonstrate active listening while maintaining eye contact.
A – cknowledge
  Show empathy not sympathy but do not agree.
R – efine
  Use listening and questioning skills to establish if the objection is real. Isolate the objection.
D – efine the objection
  State the objection back to the customer to show you understand it. Use closed questions to gain confirmation.
O – vercome the objection, or outweigh
  Demonstrate that the concern is unfounded. Restate the benefits to outweigh the objection. Use features linked to benefits to address the issues.
C – lose the sale
  Ask the customer to say 'yes' even if it's clear they have agreed.

Features and benefits

> *'Now that I am no longer president I find I no longer win every game of golf I play.'*
>
> **GEORGE BUSH SNR**
> **President of the United States of America**

The module on features and benefits equips sales teams with the ability to translate propositions associated with the business's brands/products into tangible benefits for the customer.

A customer will not say 'yes' to a proposition if it is centered on the features of a product. A feature could be such aspects as the labelling of a product, the mechanics of a particular promotional activity that is being proposed, the trading terms that accompany a specific activity and so on.

To define a benefit it is essential to have a clear comprehension of the customer's strategic priorities. That way you can target the consumers that frequent their outlet. Once the marketing team has defined an activity that will be used to support brands at the point of purchase, it is the responsibility of the sales team to translate these into customer propositions using the customer's language. Then they identify the benefits of the proposition to the customer prior to putting it in front of the buyer or key customer contact.

To bridge the gap between a feature of an activity or product that we are proposing to a customer and articulating the benefit we use link phrases.

Some examples of these are captured below.

Features may include ...	Link phrases examples ...	Benefits including ...
Based on consumer research we have changed the packaging of the product ...	... which will give you ...	... greater visibility of the major brand in the category making it more eye-catching for shoppers, driving increased consumer purchase.
In April we are conducting a television advertising campaign to create awareness of this new product ...	... leading to ...	An increased number of consumers visiting your outlet to purchase the product.
We have changed the packaging to enable you to purchase a smaller number of units at any one time.	Additionally you will have ...	... a substantial reduction in wastage.
We have changed the production location of the product ...	... which will provide you with ...	... improved profitability because the costs of goods are lower and we can pass some of this saving on to you.
As part of this proposition we can come into your stores to merchandise the product in the new display unit ...	... so that involves ...	... a reduced demand on the time of your team to implement the activity.

Key points to remember relating to features and benefits are these.

- A *feature* is part of the make up and characteristic of a product or plan.
- Convert into benefit – 'what does it do for me (the customer)?'
- Use feature – link phrase – benefit.
- A *benefit* is a favourable result upon taking certain action.
- Benefits are supported by features.
- Not all features are benefits.
- Contacts buy because of benefits, not features.
- Sales can be lost if salespeople do not sell identified benefits effectively.

Learning how to translate the features of an activity into definitive customer benefits will certainly help customers to say 'yes' more often. The chances of receiving a 'yes' are even higher if the salesperson is able to put a definitive number behind the customer benefit.

The sales teams have to use the thinking process below to convert features into definitive customer benefits.

Feature	Link phrase which means that ...	Benefit customer/consumer

Customer needs

'There is only one boss. The customer. And he can fire everybody in the company from the chairman on down, simply by spending his money somewhere else.'
SAM WALTON, American businessman

This module is about getting a detailed understanding of the strategic imperatives relating to any given customer. It centres on defining the needs of a customer and a key contact within the customer's organisation. We then match any business proposition to a definitive benefit that the customer and the key contact can instantly relate to.

In 2004 I was working with the North American business of Diageo to identify and unlock growth within the On Trade (pubs, bars, hotels, restaurants and so on). The project had many strengths, from identifying the most appropriate brands based on consumer motivations within any segment to the skills that salespeople would need to get customers to say 'yes' more often. At the very heart of the project, which was to have a significant and positive impact on both Diageo's and customer's performance, was the identification of customers' needs and how these related to all suppliers, and specifically Diageo.

There are two key ingredients in understanding the needs of customers. Firstly, it is imperative to understand the business from the retailer's perspective. This means having detailed knowledge of how the day-to-day business operates, how the retailer measures performance, and not least a clear understanding of their priorities – their primary and secondary needs.

The second key ingredient is to know very clearly 'how' customers plan to achieve their business aims. These we call the driving needs of the business. Examples of these could include increasing the number of consumers, multi-use occasions like coffee in the morning with friends, an evening meeting place over dinner, adapting their range and layout and similar initiatives.

In North America we ran a series of what could be described as 'focus groups'. We invited customers from different segments, for example Themed Food and Drink, Fine Dining and so on to join us to discuss their specific needs from suppliers. The aim of these sessions was to identify the common aspects that customers from similar segments were identifying as being crucial to their long-term success.

In Part I (Chapter 3) we looked at 'What's in it for the organisation', 'What's in it for teams' and 'What's in it for me'. Using a similar approach we developed the hierarchy of customer needs for each individual segment where we were seeking to further improve our business performance. The output from these sessions was that no two segments had the same driving needs of their business. Yes, they all had the same primary need – centred on driving profitability for their business. Secondary needs like improving margin, managing their cash and so on supported this primary need. However, the real differences emerged around how they would achieve these goals.

From this it is clear that to sell any proposition into a customer it is crucial to determine the driving needs of the customer's organisation and work out how a proposition relates to one or several of these needs. The driving needs then fuel both the supporting needs and the primary needs.

Understanding how a business plans to achieve its strategic aims is one thing. However, as we have already discovered, without connecting your proposition to the goals of individual contacts within a customer it is difficult to get them to say 'yes'. This means that we have to extend the hierarchy of customer needs beyond strategic imperatives and driving needs into the needs of the individual – their personal needs. Examples of personal needs include their need to have an appropriate work–life balance, their personal compensation package, their desire for promotion and other similar factors. Once you have identified the personal needs of your key contact and the driving needs of their organisation it is far easier to build propositions to which they say 'yes' more often. This I define as: minimising the 'connection gap' between a supplier's business and their customer's.

Here is the framework for the hierarchy of customer needs:

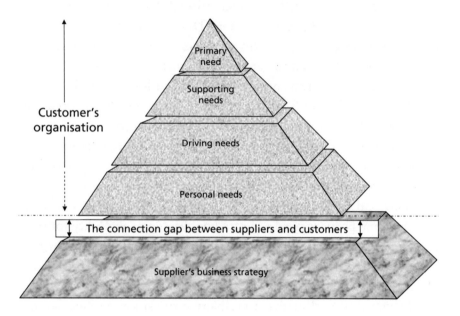

Determining the needs of customers shows us how to translate the features of products into tangible benefits for customers and individual contacts. Here are the points to remember.

- We have to identify the needs of individuals as well as the needs of our customer's business.
- We have to establish how to match our propositions to the driving needs of our customer's business.
- If we ensure that all proposals focus on the things that matter to the customer personally whilst also meeting the needs of their business, we increase the likelihood of securing a 'yes'.

Consultative selling

'I have heard of a man who had a mind to sell his house,
and therefore carried a piece of brick in his pocket, which
he shewed as a pattern to encourage purchasers.'
JONATHAN SWIFT, Irish poet and satirist

This module is relevant to every member of any sales organisation. It provides a structured format for developing persuasive commercial propositions that will benefit both the customer and the supplier's business, as it addresses the needs of both parties.

When this foundation skill is embedded within the organisation, salespeople will be able consistently to:

- understand the rationale of the consultative selling approach;
- realise the benefits of structuring commercial propositions in this format;
- understand the elements of, and information required for each of the five stages; and
- develop commercially persuasive proposals in this format.

The consultative selling methodology ensures that there is a consistent and structured way of thinking and working in preparing propositions for customers. It provides an opportunity to sell the benefits of any proposal in a compelling way, which is both sequential and logical. Being a disciplined approach it requires planning, utilising the components of communicating with customers, presenting benefits rather than features and pre-planning for any objections a customer may have. Following this approach, sales teams will be able to present a professional and highly persuasive positioning of any proposal that will lead a customer to say 'yes' more often.

It also provides the ideal structure to outline the benefits of adopting the ideas and actions associated with the planned activity or brand-building initiatives you are presenting; it enables the sales team to explain ways of, and reasons for, doing things differently. Finally, it is a win–win–win approach for the business, the customer and the consumer.

There are five key stages of the consultative selling approach.

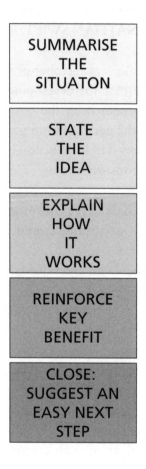

The five stages:

1 Summarise the situation

The first stage of the process aims at understanding issues and gathering information. It involves detailed research before the appointment into areas such as the key issues the customer is facing. You go over in your mind consumer and customer insights, and make sure you understand their implications. It sets the scene for the business proposal and provides relevant context and background to aid understanding of the proposal. They should be of interest to both parties.

Items covered may include:

- market situation including trends, competitor analysis and opportunities;
- brand innovation and development;
- category performance both within the customer's business and the market in general;
- customer performance in relation to the business's portfolio of products; and
- any sales building opportunities and initiatives.

The skills you need when summarising the situation include:

- active listening;
- questioning, including the use of open, closed and probing questions;
- identifying the customer's needs; and
- summarising the situation and the position of both parties.

2 State the idea

This follows on from the summary. Tailor it to the customer's needs and always indicate the anticipated financial benefit of the proposal to the customer. It should be a simple explanation, concise and clear.

When stating the idea you will:

- recognise the original issue/need of the customer;
- propose a solution for meeting both the business and individual customer's needs; and
- make quite sure that it's straightforward, logical and easy to understand.

It should cover:

- details of the benefits to the customer;
- quantification of the benefits; and
- how defined brand-building or sales-building initiatives activity will support the proposal at the consumer point of purchase.

The skills you need when stating the idea include:

- creative problem solving;
- identifying and matching customer needs; and
- communication skills.

3 Explain how it works

This gives you the opportunity to deliver a more detailed explanation of the proposition. Clarity and simplicity is important, demonstrating how the proposal matches the defined needs of both the customer and the consumer. It outlines who needs to do what, where and when. It details dates, service and the actions required to make the proposition happen as effectively as possible in order to maximise the identified benefits. Personalise the style of the explanation to accord with the style of the contact and the customer.

The skills you need when explaining how it works include:

- overcoming objections;
- listening and questioning to ensure understanding; and
- clear communication skills.

4 Reinforce key benefits

This is the time to restate the benefits of the proposal and again link it to the needs of the customer. During this stage the onus is on the salesperson to highlight the benefits in a succinct and memorable way that matches the customer's needs. Make sure it reinforces how it will support both the primary and supporting needs of the business. Summarise the benefits on a page for the contact to see.

The skills you need when reinforcing the benefit include:

- accurately summarising the proposal;
- questioning to check understanding; and
- ensuring that the message is memorable and meets the original need.

5 Close – suggest an easy next step

The next core skill of selling is that of 'closing the deal'. This fifth stage of the consultative selling process is about providing the customer with a choice. It includes defined, easy next steps. It should be compelling, i.e. easy to say 'yes' to and confirms who does what. It confirms the agreement and gains the commitment of both parties to the proposition.

It should cover:

- The proposal's benefit to both the customer and the contact; and
- an action plan for the next steps.

The skills you need during the 'close' stage include:

- practised skill at closing the deal, employing a variety of closes;
- listening and questioning; and
- the ability to place the order!

The simple screener on the next page is a useful tool to aid planning and preparation prior to presenting a proposition to customers in the consultative selling framework:

Summarise the situation Conditions? Needs? Limitations? Benefits? Confirm contact's interest	
State the idea Simple, Clear, Concise? Does it meet the needs? Does it suggest action? What is the financial benefit for the customer?	
Explain how it works Who does what, when, where? Give assurance it's practical Anticipate questions and objections Ensure understanding	
Reinforce Key Benefits Reinforce that the idea meets the needs	
Close – suggest an easy next step Offer a choice Get a decision Suggest actions for both parties.	

Closing the deal

> 'Deals are my art form. Other people paint beautifully on canvas or write wonderful poetry. I like making deals, preferable big deals. That's how I get my kicks.'
> **DONALD TRUMP, American businessman**

This module is about the final, most critical element of the selling process. A customer relationship is based on longer- as well as shorter-term interests from both sides; remember that it is a buyer's job to buy and the salesperson's job to sell. It is about getting the customer to commit to your proposition by saying 'yes'. The module identifies the various ways of closing a deal. It also looks at the follow-up to a successful close.

When this foundation skill is embedded within the organisation, salespeople will consistently be able to:

- understand why they always need to close;
- understand the different types of close;
- choose the appropriate close for any situation; and
- take the next steps after closing a deal.

Without a close there is no commitment from either side. To close effectively, timing is critical. If you feel that the time is right to make the close but have a concern that the customer may say 'no', do not delay – make the close anyway. As we discovered when reviewing the foundation skill of overcoming objections, a 'no' is often caused by a lack of understanding. In most cases you can start the process over again, finding out what elements the customer does not understand or does not feel comfortable with, then overcome or outweigh the arguments and move once again towards another close.

There are various ways to make a close. Which one is appropriate depends on the situation, the type of proposition being made and how strong the arguments are. If a proposition is not equitable there is a heightened risk of receiving a 'no' from the customer. If you have rooted the proposition in an outstanding proposal for both the customer and consumer, where all parties will receive significant benefits, then a 'yes' is far more likely.

Opinion is divided as to how many different types of close are possible within the sales arena. With our clients we suggest there are eight – yes, eight – different types of close, all used in varying contexts.

1 Summary close

Summarise the key points from the meeting and recommend action:
'So to summarise the key points of the proposition ... Have I missed anything? ... Well then, I suggest ...'

2 Assumptive close

After the presentation, close straight away, assuming the customer will agree:

> '*In view of our discussions, I will arrange for the order to be sent next Monday.*'

3 Alternative close

Let the customer choose between two or more positive alternatives:

> '*Would you like the order to be delivered this week or next week?*'

4 Special benefits close

Point out the benefit of agreeing now:

> '*If you order today it will be delivered at pre-price increase … terms that will become effective at the end of next week.*'

5 Fear close

Point out the risks of missing the opportunity if they do not decide now:

> '*If you are unable to order today we cannot guarantee delivery of the promotion packs as stocks are running down.*'

6 Minor point close

Build agreement on a number of minor points before the major one:

> '*You know that our product is the fastest growing within the category. You keep going out of stock and losing valuable sales opportunities … therefore I have adjusted your standard order to prevent this and so we will deliver an extra ten cases per week.*'

7 Reference close

Reference the performance of other customers who have accepted a similar proposition:

> *'Customer x has seen an x% uplift in sales as a result of running this particular promotional activity.'*

8 Concession close

Start with higher figures and agree to reduce in line with the customer's expectations or needs:

> *'I shall send two pallets per outlet with three for larger stores. Is that OK?'*

Once a customer has said 'yes' to a proposal it is important to summarise the understanding of the agreement and to play this back to the customer. It is critical that both parties are agreeing to the same thing. Once this is done, then review the implications of the deal. Do this through agreeing the action points making sure you cover who does what, where and when.

After you have concluded the agreement, obtained a signature and left the customer, no doubt punching the air when you have got off the premises, then complete the follow-up swiftly.

Follow-up actions include the following.

- Confirming the agreement in writing.
- Checking that all defined actions have been assigned.
- Dispatching orders using the appropriate logistics.
- Updating the customer record card.
- Updating outlet/customer objectives.
- Sending a note to other departments in your business where appropriate.
- Reviewing performance in the call; did I achieve the call objectives, what I could do differently next time (and so on)?

Then manage the agreement, ensuring that the assigned people are following all the action points agreed with the customer. Make sure that people are held accountable for their areas of responsibility in delivering the agreement.

There are six rules to managing any agreement with a customer:

1   police the agreement;
2   ensure you keep your side;
3   ensure that there are not any defaulters to the agreement;
4   react quickly if anything does not go to plan;
5   recognise and reward the contribution of others; and
6   renegotiate with the customer if commitments are not honoured on time, letting the customer know in advance if you cannot meet a commitment.

> ' All right, but apart from sanitation, medicine, education, wine, public order, irrigation, roads, the fresh water system, and public health, what have the Romans ever done for us?'
> 'Brought peace?'
> 'Oh, peace, shut up.'
>
> **MONTY PYTHON,** Life of Brian

Selling is the art of helping people to say 'yes' to propositions more often. The foundation skills of selling are a prerequisite in any business that builds sustainable profit through customers. Essential to building a successful relationship with customers in the long term is not only knowing the foundation skills, but ensuring that every proposition delivers benefits to all stakeholders; your business, the customer and the consumer. Businesses only achieve this when these foundation skills are embedded into the DNA of the sales organisation. These have to be trained, coached and nurtured at all times to ensure that not one, but every proposition is developed, presented, executed, measured and evaluated with excellence. In so doing 'the train has left the station' towards the destination of turning your sales force into profit heroes.

Key learnings	That's interesting

Action plan	
What could I do?	
Who would it involve?	
When should I aim to have it done by?	
What resources or dependencies are involved?	

PACKAGING THE SKILLS TO EQUIP THE ORGANISATION

6

'An expert is someone who knows some of the worst mistakes that can be made in his subject and who manages to avoid them.'

WERNER HEISENBERG, German mathematical physicist

The operating standards of a sales team and their understanding of the components of core skills they need to exhibit do not on their own demonstrate a point of differentiation in the eyes of customers. That comes from how thoroughly these capabilities and skills are embedded and exhibited: that comes from equipping the sales teams with superb customer propositions that support brands, and products with broad consumer connectivity.

My perspective on best practice is to equip line managers with the content, tools and skills to coach their direct reportees. In Part III we will turn our focus onto building the capability of line managers to both train and coach. I will explain how we must equip managers with the skills to achieve maximum engagement, retention and recall around any given subject, and to ensure that their teams exhibit the defined skills on a day-to-day basis.

A modular approach to building capability means that you can train and coach people in bite-sized chunks. For our clients to do their own training we package the core skills into smaller modules they can cascade as part of team meetings. The benefits of this are that it minimises the time that sales teams are 'off the road', ensures that individuals are not overloaded with content and allows time for them to digest and practise the given skill prior to building their personal capability library further.

In this chapter we will:

- examine the journey to build capability of a sales team; and
- define the methodologies required to package content, making it come to life for the audience.

Building capability is a journey not a destination

'When embarking on a polar exhibition, begin with a clear idea which pole you are dashing at, and try to start facing the right way.'
W. C. SELLAR and R. J. YEATMAN, authors

Many academics and sales professionals have eulogised over the skills of effective salespeople. I believe effective salespeople are those who can connect passionately with their customers, building sustainable win–win partnerships. There are varying approaches to building capability; however, our focus here is on equipping sales teams with the core skills with which they can embark on the journey of becoming leading sales professionals. This journey culminates in achieving outstanding relationships with customers through joint and strategic working where the focus of both the supplier and the customer is on achieving growth for both parties.

No matter how far one is intending to travel, every journey starts with a single step. For us this first step is translated into embedding the core skills of the sales team. The skills continue to evolve along with the changing needs of clients.

In Chapter 2 we reflected on the challenge faced by the international brewing giant in Eastern Europe. The challenge they were facing was how to embed a common way of selling within a multi-faceted, multi-lingual business. Having determined the shape and construct of three elements (skills, knowledge and behaviour) we embarked on packaging these into bite-sized chunks, starting with the foundation skills of the sales teams. This methodology we find has relevance whatever the commodity, culture or indeed geography of the organisation.

In Chapter 5 I defined the core skills to sell exceptional brands. A module centred on embedding the most appropriate structured call or appointment supplements these skills.

- Communicating with customers
- Handling objections
- Features and benefits

- Customer needs
- Consultative selling
- Closing the deal
- Structured call or appointment.

There is no right or wrong answer as to the most appropriate sequence in which to coach these skills. This depends on the defined needs of the team. Once you have established the required operational standards, developed role profiles and then assessed individuals on their current level of the skills appropriate to their role, you can identify the priority development opportunities at both an individual and team level. Recognising that the consistency of approach is vital will ensure that you establish a common way of selling. Customers will recognise and embrace the common approach, no matter who the individual is with whom they are interacting.

We have established that individuals start the learning process with differing levels of skills and experience. The goal is to ensure that everyone understands and exhibits the same standards during interactions with customers. It is therefore right and relevant to ensure that teams are all coached in these fundamental principles.

No approaches to the content of core skills are exactly the same for any two organisations. However, we have broken down these skills into modules of similar size. I recommend that they are all designed as interactive learning experiences where individuals step into the spotlight to take responsibility for their own learning. As we discovered, Professor Gardner identified that there are eight primary ways in which people learn; consequently, materials have to be packaged in such a way as to appeal to as many of these learning preferences as possible.

Once the framework of each skill has been established for the whole organisation, it is then the responsibility of the individual business unit or line manager to customise the learning for their team. This could include inserting, in pre-determined slots, examples of local application or relevance. It could also include translating materials into different languages, or even making adaptations based on the existing mean capability of the individuals to whom the skill is to be cascaded.

Line managers do not deliver the core skills in one-day or even half-day modules. They receive the training broken down into bite-sized chunks. The average length of time it takes to train each of the individual modules initially to a team of approximately ten to twelve learners is shown in the table below.

Module	Time
Communicating with customers	1 hour 50 minutes
Handling objections	1 hour 30 minutes
Features and benefits	1 hour
Customer needs	1 hour
Consultative selling	2 hours 5 minutes
Closing the deal	1 hour 5 minutes
Structured call or appointment	1 hour 55 minutes

I recommend groups of ten to twelve people, the reason being that, in our experience, these are the optimum group sizes in order to gain full participation from all the attendees, balanced against the appropriate size of audience for one line manager to coach. In saying that, it is unusual for a line manager to have as many direct reports as this. It allows for line managers to buddy up with a peer, to drive capability across more than one team at the same time. Added to the obvious benefit of time effectiveness, teams interact in the learning environment, building relationships beyond their immediate peer group.

The challenge then is to make the material relevant for the business, the team and individuals.

Packaging modules

*'The struggle of man against power is the struggle of
memory against forgetting.'*
MILAN KUNDERA, Czech novelist

One of the biggest criticisms I have of some organisations is that of
corporate memory loss. They define ways of working, they establish
capability building blocks and cascade them into the organisation.
They determine these by initiatives and opportunities at a point of
time to allow the organisation to do any number of things, including
outperforming the competition, growing market share, responding to
the changing demands of customers, embracing innovative solutions
and so forth. One thing is for certain, and that is that any individual
or team who have had the responsibility of establishing the capability
building blocks will at some stage, like everyone else, leave the organisation. Organisations commonly put little focus on ensuring that what
is created has a lasting legacy, although there is no doubt that the core
content will need to evolve over time.

You must package materials and content in a way that ensures
that the business will easily understand it in the longer term. Having
materials without detailed speaker notes, opportunities for extended
learning or resilience to changing business dynamics will ultimately
mean that they need to be rewritten in the future.

For any skills module I recommend a number of components.

- Programme objectives and session construct
- Trainer manual
- Participant manual
- Learning log book
- Supporting tools and materials
- Self-assessment screener
- Learning extensions.

In order to demonstrate how these materials come together I am using
the construct of a number of modules. This will demonstrate how

to package content so as to ensure that it has lasting relevance to an organisation.

Programme objectives and session construct

> *'There exists a great chasm between those, on one side, who relate everything to a single central vision ... and, on the other side, those who pursue many ends, often unrelated and even contradictory.'*
>
> **ISAIAH BERLIN, British philosopher**

There are two elements to defining programme objectives and session construct. Prior to building the detailed content, it is crucial to engage all stakeholders with the learning objectives associated with the subject. To facilitate this, I recommend completing a curriculum subject screener. This will ensure that everyone in the organisation is aligned with the topic of the module, the learning objectives associated with it, key aspects of the proposed content and the target audiences within the business.

This is an example of a screener that we used with one of our clients to gain alignment around a module on closing the deal:

Curriculum subject:

Close the deal

What is the module about

This module is about the final and most critical step in the selling process; Close the Deal. This is the moment when you ask the customer to accept the proposition.

This module will look at the various ways a deal can be closed and key points about closing the deal in general. The module will also look at the administrative part of closing the deal; the follow-up and management of the agreed points.

Learning objectives

After completing this module delegates will be able to:
- *Understand why a close is always needed*
- *Understand what the different types of closures are*
- *Decide what type of closure is most appropriate in which situation*
- *Know what the next steps are after the deal is closed*

Key aspects of the proposed content

- *Types of closures*
- *When to utilise what type of closure*
- *Key points of Close the Deal*
- *Concluding the agreement*
- *Follow up*
- *Managing the agreement*

Target audience(s)

Sales: *SM / RSM / ASM / NKAcM / KACM*
Trade Marketing:
Marketing:
Training: *STM / ST*

This document outlines the key objectives and content for the above module.

Please:
- *Provide any existing best practice from within the business either locally or centrally, content which you believe needs to be referenced within this module.*
- *Sign off this document to enable us to proceed with the development of the module.*
- *Return the signed document and supporting / additional materials by x date.*

Signed: Date:

Once we have defined the scope of a given subject and identified good practice around our customer's organisation we then develop the module.

The programme outline defines the overall content and running order. As well as determining the time each component will take, it also summarises the resources required for a session and what both the trainer and learners are doing at any given point in time. We use the template below to develop the programme outline.

This becomes a key tool for trainers to prepare themselves to deliver a learning session to their teams as well as being the key navigation tool when running a learning session.

Time for the topic	Topic or chunk of learning	What resources are required for the session e.g. posters, breakout materials, presentation slide(s) and so on?	What is the trainer doing during this part of the learning experience?	What are the learners doing during this part of the learning experience?
5 mins	Module objectives	Poster – What's in it for me & what's in it for our customers? Presentation slide. Learner notebooks	Referring to the poster: ask individuals to turn to the person next to them to discuss what they believe the content of the module could be and the benefits to themselves and their customers. Capturing ideas in their learner notebooks. Asking for pairs to share their thoughts and observations. Summarising the objectives of the module through a presentation slide and allowing learners to add to their notes	Looking at the poster. Listening to the brief for the short exercise. Discussing with their partners and capturing notes in their learner notebook. Sharing with the group. Listening and capturing any additional module objectives in their learner notebooks
Add rows for each chunk of learning which can be broken down into anything between 5-minute and 30-minute sections.				

Trainer manual

> *'Parenthood is a lot easier to get into than out of.'*
> **BRUCE LANSKY, author and publisher**

The trainer manual provides whoever is facilitating a learning session with everything they need to know in order to run the module successfully with their group of learners.

It commences with an overview of the module and defines the learning objectives. It identifies to whom the module is relevant, and suggests other aspects of individual development that should have been completed by learners prior to attending this particular session.

The session construct then follows, sharing with them the 'running order' of the session. The construct includes the time each component should take, along with the resources required and the roles for themselves and their learners.

The construction of the manual allows trainers to spend time preparing themselves for the session. It clearly lays out what they need to say at any stage, which materials support each section, as well as communicating a number of tips on how they can enhance the learning experience as they journey through the module.

Here is an example of a few pages out of a trainer manual on identifying customer's needs.

Trainer overview of the module

This module is about identifying customer needs and fully understanding the commercial objectives of the customer. The module considers the customer's strategic issues and the tactical activities they are using to deliver those strategies. Identifying Customer Needs is founded on understanding the things that are important to the customer.

This module is supported by the 'Needs Matrix' which challenges us to consider the commercial activities that the customer believes will deliver their financial and strategic goals. The 'Needs Matrix' can be applied for any customer. There are tools that help us to understand the customer's Strategy and Tactics and also the way that customers measure success. Using these tools enables us to identify our key customer's needs.

The module references basic questioning and active listening skills as a key skill required to identify customer needs. These skills are covered in more detail in separate modules

This module applies and supports the 'Integrated Sales Model' because it promotes collaboration and win–win solutions.

Module objectives

After completing this module delegates will be able to:
- *clearly define customer needs and the benefits of identifying them;*
- *focus their business proposals to incorporate the needs that are important to their customer;*
- *use the 'Needs Matrix' for all customers;*
- *use tools that will enable them to understand how customers measure success;*
- *explore strategic implications that will influence their customer's decision-making; and*
- *review their listening and questioning skills.*

Prerequisites

To benefit the most from this module, the participants should already be familiar with, and have completed the following modules.
- *Listening and Questioning*
- *Steps of a Call.*

Module outline

Module steps	Timing (mins)
1 Module Overview/Objectives	5
2 Group discussion & Exercise 'Identifying the Skills Required'	10
3 Group discussion 'Defining Needs and Benefits'	5
4 Group discussion – More Customer Needs	5
5 The Needs Triangle – Briefing the task	5
6 Task: Completing the Needs Matrix	15
7 The Needs Triangles – Reviewing model answers	15
8 Introduction to Strategic Considerations	10
9 How customers measure success	10
10 Task briefing and running – Pulling it all together	25
11 Review of the Task – Pulling it all together	10
12 Summary – What have we learned?	5
13 Questions and Discussion	5
Total Time	2 hrs 5mins

Trainer note:

At the dotted line you can break up this module into shorter sessions and deliver them over time. If you use this option remember to adjust your materials. Also, it will take additional set-up time each time you begin a new session.

Activity	Activity explanation
PRESENT Slide 1	Identifying Customer Needs Present visual aid slide number one

Step 1: Module Overview/objectives .... 5 minutes

Activity	Activity explanation
SAY	Welcome to Identifying Customer Needs This module focuses on identifying customer needs and fully understanding the commercial objectives of the customer. The module helps us to identify things that are important to the customer. We shall be exploring a number of tools that focus on the commercial activities that deliver the customer's financial and strategic goals. The module is applicable to all customers.

Trainers should use the trainer manual, not only to prepare for the session but throughout any learning event to assist them in covering the subject matter to the very best of their ability. In all modular skills sessions there are times when learners will be engaged on an aspect of learning without requiring the direct input of the trainer/line manager. This provides the trainer with the opportunity to briefly recap with the manual to ensure that they have covered the relevant content to date and refresh themselves on any sections still to follow.

Participant manual

> *'Today is the tomorrow you worried about yesterday.'*
> **MARK TWAIN, American writer**

The participant manual is not dissimilar to the trainer manual. It allows learners not only to follow the session in one of Gardner's relevant learning preferences, e.g. linguistic, intrapersonal, logical/mathematical, visual/spatial (see Chapter 2); but also to act as a reference guide once they have completed any learning session. Research has shown that it is not uncommon for individuals to remember only ten per cent of what someone says to them. The participant manual will reinforce learning and allow individuals to recall the content far more accurately at a later date.

Here is an example of a few pages out of a participant manual on Communicating with Customers.

What is this module about?

This module is about communicating with customers more effectively and efficiently through building rapport, effective listening and questioning, and through adapting your style and approach to the attitude and interpersonal style of the customer.

This module takes a structured approach to questioning by looking at the different types of questions and how to use them effectively to make a point to the customer, developing the conversation. The module looks at the keys to good listening and at what can go wrong when you are listening. The module also looks at verbal and non-verbal buying signals and the importance of body language. Finally, we look at the different interpersonal styles customers may have and how to deal most effectively with them.

The tool created for making propositions to the customer, the 'Developing the Conversation Template', supports this module. This tool helps you to follow a structured and effective approach when making customer propositions. The second tool, the 'Style Identifier Matrix', helps you to identify the natural style of your customer and allows you to adapt your own style and behaviour accordingly.

This module applies to and supports the 'Integrated Sales Model' because it forms the foundation and starting point of any customer interaction.

Learning objectives

After completing this module you will be able to:
* *Listen and question more effectively when interacting with customers.*
* *Use a structured approach when making propositions to customers.*

- *Recognise and identify the different personal styles customers have.*
- *Adapt your own behaviour based on the customer's natural style.*

Picture of slide that is presented on screen at this stage

Ice breaker

We are starting this training module with a little breakout exercise. This exercise will help you get in the mood of the subject of communicating with customers and at the same time give you an insight into your own natural communication style.

We would like you to do the exercise in threes. Each of you takes turns playing the salesperson, the customer and the observer.

When it is your turn to be the salesperson we would like you to choose something you want to sell to the customer. This should not be business- or category-related.

As a salesperson you need to influence the customer in a way that you would normally do. As the customer we would like you to play a little 'difficult-to-influence'. As an observer we would like you to take note of how many times the salesperson makes a statement (gives information) and how many times the salesperson asks a question (seeks information).

After 3 minutes, the exercise should stop and you should change roles. Each time, the observer takes note of how many times the salesperson makes a statement and how many times they ask a question.

After each participant has played all three roles during 3 minutes, each of you will share among your group for the salesperson you have observed, how many times the salesperson made a statement (gave information) and how many times the salesperson asked a question (sought information).

This is an exercise to learn what your natural style as a salesperson is. If you as a salesperson gave information more than 5 times as much as seeking information, you have a strong 'push' style. A ratio of between 3–5 to 1 indicates a moderate push style, and a ratio of between 1–3 to 1 is an average level. If you sought information more times than you gave information, then you have a natural 'pull' style.

The participant manual is given to all learners at the start of a session.

Learning logbook

> *'What's another word for thesaurus?'*
> **STEVEN WRIGHT, American stand-up comedian,**
> **actor and writer**

Being able to personalise your learning is critical to assisting in both engagement and recall. A learning logbook allows individuals to capture their own thoughts at any time under broad visual descriptors of content chunks contained within a module. It normally takes the form of a bound document containing between ten and twelve pages, depending on the size of the module. Each page has visual stimulation to guide learners on where the appropriate space could be for them to capture any points that are relevant to them on their learning journey.

We heavily encourage trainers, as well as learners, to use a learning logbook. For trainers it can be the place for them to capture any stories or anecdotes they may wish to use to enhance the learning session and create greater relevance. They can also use it to capture any notes that would either fuel their personal confidence when running the session, or remind them of key points that they may wish to make. The key benefit of trainers using a learning logbook is that they are also modelling the behaviour that they are encouraging from their learners. Remember: an effective session is about collective learning and inclusivity, not one person telling and a group listening.

On the following page is an example of a page from a learning logbook that we have used with one of our clients. Learners can capture any relevant thoughts within their logbook, for example: 'I need to determine the customer needs for Niall's supermarkets as this will help me develop more appropriate propositions' and so on.

The key is for them to be very visual allowing for individual interpretation with plenty of room for jotting down; or even better, for attaching sticky notes which they can move around the book as they feel appropriate.

Spotlight on the learner

My customer

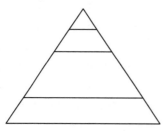 

Supporting tools and materials

> *'Give us the tools and we will finish the job.'*
> **WINSTON CHURCHILL, British Conservative statesman,**
> **Prime Minister**

The supporting tools and materials vary considerably depending on the individual module. They comprise a number of components.

1   Generally there is a presentation format that the trainer can project on to a screen to the whole learning group. Never fill these with lots of words: they generally perform one of three functions. Firstly, they are general navigation points allowing learners to know where they are in the learning process. Secondly, they are really effective for briefing a task, exercise or breakout exercise. Trainers share the instructions with the group and then leave them on the screen for learners to see and reacquaint themselves with the task in hand. Thirdly, they anchor, or summarise, any specific chunk of learning.

2   Trainers position hand-drawn posters around the learning environment. The posters are framed with a line round them to focus the eye and hung a little crooked to help oxygenate the brain. These emphasise a key point from the content. There is always a reference to them in the trainer manual to ensure that the trainer refers to the learning of each poster at some stage during the session.

3   There may be materials to support breakout exercises; they can include both props and information sheets.

4   There will be a standard summary of equipment required to run a session detailing everything from a projector to pens for flip charts.

5   There are often electronic tools and templates which sales teams will be able to take away to use to improve the application of the given subject.

The key point for trainers is to remember that it takes planning, preparation and practice to run any engagement session with their team. This not only involves tailoring the subject matter to the learners' needs and becoming very familiar with the content but also ensuring that all the material required to run a successful session are at hand.

Self-assessment screener

> '*Examine for a moment an ordinary mind on an ordinary day.*'
>
> **VIRGINIA WOOLF, English novelist**

The self-assessment screener allows learners to ascertain their level of learning at the end of any session. It is self-facilitated. In other words, it is not something that they have to hand in for marking, causing the personal dread of wondering how well they got on. Once it has been completed the trainer then shares the answers with all the learners. So it is not a test. It allows them to determine for themselves how well they have grasped the content during the course of the session and understand what further learning opportunities they may have on the subject. It also provides information for them to share with their line manager, if they want to, on areas of personal development associated with this skill. They can use it to identify areas on which they wish to solicit feedback from their line manager during their next joint meetings with customers.

This is an example of a screener we have used in relation to Steps of a Call with one of our clients.

	Steps of a call Self-assessment tool	
	Name: _____ Position: _____ Line Manager: _____ Date: _____	
	Please answer the questions below to assess your understanding of this module:	
Q1	Which of these statements is incorrect?	
	Structured calling saves time for customers	
	Structured calling saves time for x (business name)	
	Structured calling takes more time but it's worth it	
	Structured calling is more professional	
Q2	What is the fourth step in the x (business name) Steps of a Call?	
	Sales Presentation	
	Close the Order	
	Take Action	
	Approach & Check	
Q3	When preparing the Steps of a Call which of the following is incorrect?	
	Review outlet records	
	Check selling tools	
	Revise your journey plan	
	Review outlet objectives	
Q4	Which of these activities is not part of the Approach and Check?	
	Greeting the customer staff	
	Following up on outstanding queries	

	Checking the outlet selling areas	
	Checking the outlet stock room area	
Q5	Which of the following actions is not part of stock replenishment?	
	Stock from the last stock take	
	Stock that has been cancelled from the order	
	Stock ordered during the last visit	
	Stock remaining in the outlet	
Q6	Which of the following closes is an assumptive close?	
	Key points of the meeting and actions agreed	
	Not asking for the order but outlining the next steps in delivery	
	Providing the customer with a choice of actions	
	Building agreement to minor points	
Q7	Which of the following closes is an alternative close?	
	Key points of the meeting and actions agreed	
	Not asking for the order but outlining the next steps in delivery	
	Providing the customer with a choice of actions	
	Building agreement to minor points	
Q8	When Taking Action, what should you not?	
	Merchandise stock from the stock room/area	
	Outline the details of your proposal	
	Merchandise stock in the cooler	
	Place display units in the selling area	

Q9	Which of the following statements is untrue when Evaluating the Call?	
	It enables more focused objective setting	
	It takes extra time	
	It enhances performance	
	It provides information for later calls	
Q10	Which of the following is not considered a selling tool	
	S M A R T Objectives	
	Market Knowledge	
	Product Knowledge	
	Product Samples	
	Total	
	Percentage	

If you are as curious as me you will be no doubt wondering what the correct answers were for this example! Well, they are:

Q1)3, Q2)2, Q3)3, Q4)2, Q5) 2, Q6) 2, Q7) 3, Q8) 2, Q9) 2, Q10)1.

It is, however, important to note that the answers may differ dependent on the client for whom we have developed the screener.

Learning extensions

> '*Don't worry about being slow; only worry about standing still. A slow progress holds some promise, to stand still promises failure.*'
>
> **Chinese proverb**

Providing learners with ways to extend their learning is critical. Remember: we all enter any learning experience with different levels of both skills and experience. We learn at differing speeds and have varying learning preferences.

I shared with you previously how the environment at school did not match my personal learning preferences. A more broadly embraced approach to packaging learning, as we have been discovering, would certainly have contained far more appeal to me. However, there would still be ways that I could further explore my learning beyond the formal session.

In Part III we will look at how to develop the rounded skills of line managers in order to embed skill beyond the training environment. For now, we have to recognise that we need to guide learners in how they can extend their learning beyond the core content on any given subject.

There are many ways in which this can be done, and here are a few.

- Recommended reading lists.
- Electronic learning environments: these can be internally developed e-learning modules through to further recommended learning available via designated internet-based sites.
- Creating self-facilitated 'buddies' among learners to share thoughts and ideas after the learning event.
- Handy hints and tips sheets for salespeople to use on a daily basis.
- 360° feedback from managers, peers, subordinates and even customers.

Why is the way that learning is packaged so important?

'When people come to ask one for help they are as warm as spring rain; when one goes to ask others for help they are as cold as frost in winter. It is easier to give help than to get it.'
Chinese proverb

Not only do line managers need the skills and confidence to train their teams; they also need the tools to achieve maximum engagement, retention and recall to the subject from their teams.

Like the core skills of selling, the components of packaging skills cannot stand on their own. Each one forms a vital component in the learning environment. There are no short cuts to implementation. Planning and preparation of the individual modules is as vital as the way that the line managers prepare to train their teams. The benefits, though, can be quite remarkable. My experience indicates that the enjoyment, learning and work applicability ratings from learners when being taught in this fashion outstrips any other methodology we have seen. In a similar way as outstanding brands with broad consumer appeal do not enjoy their potential without a great sales team, so skill development of teams does not succeed without both the best available content and great packaging of materials.

We have now identified that salespeople need clearly established operating standards. That managers need to assess them against the capability required to perform to their maximum potential. That managers need to nurture the core skills of the team through training and coaching. That there needs to be a common way of selling across the whole of the organisation.

We have identified how to develop the contents of capability to empower trainers. With outstanding brands and products supported by superb customer/consumer insights and marketing programmes, we are left with only one ingredient to turn your salespeople into profit heroes. In Part III we will identify how to equip line managers with the skills not only to train their teams but also to coach the capabilities every hour of every day.

Key learnings	That's interesting

Action plan	
What could I do?	
Who would it involve?	
When should I aim to have it done by?	
What resources or dependencies are involved?	

Part III

My line manager is my coach and mentor

INSPIRATIONAL SALES LEADERSHIP

7

'Some people think football is a matter of life and death ... I can assure them it is much more serious than that.'

BILL SHANKLY, Scottish footballer and manager of Liverpool FC

A proven capacity as a great salesperson is not enough to make the tricky transition from being a member of a sales team to being the leader of a sales team. You require additional attributes to motivate and coach a team to excellence. Nurture your capabilities in areas such as strategic capability, performance management, and cross-functional awareness. There are many others.

Take the world of football. It is no longer possible to go from being a great player to being the manager of a team. A player needs a whole series of coaching qualifications from recognised federations in order to make the move from a member of a team to a leader of a club. Yes, you will benefit from having been a great player but knowing how to get the best out of a group is quite different from excelling in your position on the field of play no matter how dedicated you might be. You have to understand off-field issues such as nutrition and fitness; you need a deep understanding of the rules and regulations involved in managing a club, and exposure to best practices. Above all you have to practise and consistently demonstrate these attributes under the watchful eyes of experts.

The transition from great salesperson to the leader of a sales team bears many similarities to the football example. There are additional dimensions required to manage a business unit instead of, for example, a group of key accounts. Not least of these are the skills required to coach a team to deliver outstanding collective performance.

In the world of sales there are three key elements to being a great coach. In this chapter we will discover the first two of these:

- the skills and capabilities to coach a team; and
- the ability to coach sales teams during a sales call when you accompany a member of your team.

The third element we will discover in the next chapter, where we will turn our focus on the skills a line manager needs to train their teams and ensure maximum engagement, retention and recall on any subject matter. Only when sales leaders consistently and effectively apply these three capabilities with their team can they hope that their team will recognise them as both a coach and a mentor.

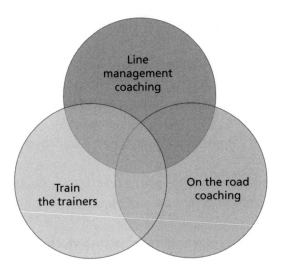

If you are going to hold line managers accountable for the training and development of their teams it is essential to equip them with the skills to do this, and you must do it effectively and consistently using a common methodology across the business.

Line management coaching

'Leadership means making people feel good.'
JEAN CHRÉTIEN, Canadian Liberal statesman

Coaching capability equips line managers with the necessary skills, techniques and tools to support their teams on a routine basis. It is a development programme for managers who are accountable for raising the performance of others. While our focus here is on the sales arm of an organisation, this skill is equally applicable across many varying functions within any business.

The content contains and explains basic coaching techniques. It provides you with tools and checklists that give the individuals responsible for coaching the opportunity to practise and obtain feedback from colleagues on their performance as a coach.

After completing this programme, line managers are able to:

- understand the principles of coaching;
- understand what an effective coach does and is responsible for;
- objectively observe and judge performance against described guidelines;
- identify and communicate performance improvement opportunities;
- use recognised models for giving feedback and setting goals; and
- complete a coaching review and objective-setting form.

We package coaching into a short initial introductory programme that the line manager's manager then revisits at frequent intervals.

Module steps	Timing (mins)
1 Learning Objectives & Overview	10
2 Principles of Coaching and the Effective Coach	5
3 The Coaching Circle – Assess Performance	5
4 The Coaching Circle – Identify the Gap	5
5 The Coaching Circle – Give Feedback	10
6 The Coaching Circle – Agree Actions	5
7 The Coaching Circle – Set Objectives	5
8 Coaching Tools	10
9 Pulling It All Together	20
10 What Have We Learned?	5
Total Time	1 hr 20

The purpose of coaching is to ensure that individuals are capable of delivering their roles effectively on behalf of the business, from making an effective structured call with customers to fulfilling all of the requirements of their role profile. It is the role of the coach to ensure that they have the right skills and understanding to be able to do this consistently. The coach's role is to identify any gaps in performance that may exist and coach the salesperson to fill the gaps.

Coaching is important to any business for a variety of reasons, because it:

- maintains and improves team and individual capability;
- supports the achievement of business objectives;
- addresses personal development opportunities;
- motivates individuals within the manager's team;
- creates a consistency of approach;
- reduces turnover within the sales function, as individuals can see that the organisation focuses on their personal development;
- ensures that work does not stop whilst the learning takes place; and
- improves the effectiveness of relationships with customers.

With this as a background it is reasonable to suggest that coaching should be a mandatory activity for any successful business.

There are four guides to being an effective coach.

1   The coaching circle;
2   Behavioural principles;
3   Giving effective feedback;
4   Planning coaching interventions.

1 The coaching circle

We use the EDIC model (Explanation/Demonstration/Imitation/Consolidation) as the basis for all coaching:

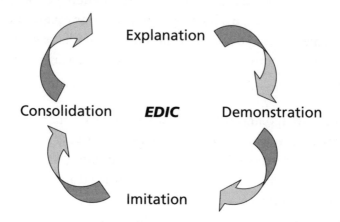

Explanation
Tell the individual what is expected of them. This means taking the time to ensure that the salesperson being coached understands the subject matter. If necessary, take the time to explain it once again and check for understanding with open questions, e.g. 'what do you think that means in practice?'

Demonstration
Show the person what you, as a coach, mean or what a given standard looks like when completed properly. The coach should be prepared to role-play to demonstrate the point if necessary.

Imitation
Let the coachees try it for themselves. Make sure that they are comfortable prior to moving to the consolidation phase.

Consolidation
This is where the coach gives feedback to the coachee. Ask the coachee to review their personal performance before you, as coach, share your

observations. Observations on performance should always start with a positive view on how the given task was completed.

2 Behavioural principles

When coaching, there are four key aspects to the behaviour of the coach. These are:

1   Being patient;
2   Being considerate;
3   Being enthusiastic;
4   Being objective.

Put the coachee at the centre of the learning for the time that you are with them. Focus has to be completely on the coaching session – distractions should be discouraged at all times. These can include simple things such as agreeing not to review e-mail on hand-held devices, nor to make phone calls and so on. Enthusiasm is infectious; if the coach is committed to making a really positive difference the coachee will be correspondingly more responsive. Finally, it is imperative to be objective and not let coaching sessions become personal: it's the behaviour you are trying to change, not the person.

3 Giving effective feedback

There are several principles associated with giving feedback, which ensure that the messages are clear, adopted by the coachee and consequently practised.

- The coach should ensure that they are not judging the individual, only the task being completed.
- Ensure that feedback is timely and is given as close in time to the actual observation of performance.
- Feedback has to be confidential to the coachee, given in private and never in front of another person.

4 Planning coaching interventions

Detailed planning is required for any coaching intervention. This starts with undertaking a thorough review of the individual's role description, training record, actions from previous coaching sessions and understanding their performance against relevant objectives. Setting realistic goals for a coaching session is important to maintain focus against specific themes or areas; in other words, do not plan to coach against too many areas in one session.

So we can summarise what an effective coach does into six key areas. An effective coach:

1   analyses learning needs. Do this objectively against the role profile and the standards of performance.
2   sets challenging standards and goals. Stretching, but realistic, to ensure that the coachee see them as 'do-able' as well as challenging.
3   appraises performance systematically. Use self-analysis to involve the coachee and achieve commitment to the identified task. Work in a routine that the coachee recognises.
4   helps a coachee to plan their functional development. Coaches are aware of and concerned with the wider development of the individual. They have read the training development file and understand the wider personal development goals of the individual. The coachee must see the coach as being helpful, interested and caring.
5   gives feedback skilfully. Involve the coachee in the process. Remain positive and encouraging but objective, to ensure that all messages are correctly understood. Provide feedback on the things that are done well as well as the potential improvement areas.
6   uses the working environment to coach. Save time by ensuring that the coaching is 'on the job'. This makes it real, as it concerns the way the coachee performs their duties and is not seen as theoretical.

The coaching circle explained

Coaching is an ongoing process. It builds and is continuous. We call this the coaching circle to which there are five key elements.

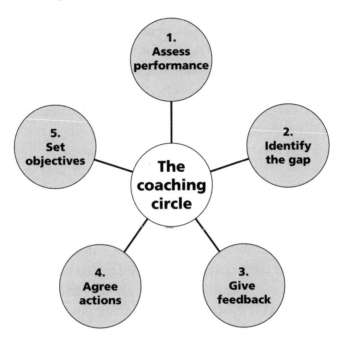

Step 1: Assess performance

This has to be objective and done against the required company standard for the task. To assess performance the coach must observe the team member; heard about second or third hand is not good enough. The coachee should know the standards and the coach should reiterate these prior to any coaching session. Going over the standards is part of a planned coaching session.

The coach has to use open questions to involve the coachee and assist them in assessing their personal performance. These could include:

'Why do you think that happened?'
'Why do you think we got that reaction from the customer?'
'What did you feel when that occurred?'

Step 2: Identify the gap

The gap is the difference between the standard for a task and the demonstrated performance that you observe.

The coachee has to be encouraged to rate their own performance, focusing on the strengths exhibited as well as the opportunities for improvement. This ensures that the coachee owns the gap. View the gap as a training need and not necessarily a reflection of the individual's ability to perform their role. The coach should use inclusive language, for example: 'How could we have approached the subject differently?', to depersonalise the feedback, as it supports the coachee and implies that they are part of the learning process.

Step 3: Give feedback

Giving feedback is a crucial skill that any coach must learn. Feedback is the vehicle for describing the level of performance and communicating the things that the coachee is doing well or needs to improve.

The process must identify something good or done well about the performance; then the coach should talk about the areas needing improvement and close with another positive point. This is often referred to as the 'Hamburger' or 'Praise Sandwich'.

For example:

'Your introduction was excellent and you quickly gained rapport with the buyer and her needs (Praise). We need to spend more time on the outlet floor to ensure that we note all the competitor activity, as that would have helped you when identifying additional visibility opportunities (Coach). You then effectively closed the deal by offering an alternative delivery date whilst assuming that the order was forthcoming without actually asking for it (Praise) ... well done! Now let's look at the learnings for the next call.'

We have looked at these areas already but they are important enough to repeat.

The coach has to create the right environment as soon as possible after the event. Making sure they are uninterrupted; keep it confidential with clear objectives.

The coach has to be clear and only talk about actual, observed behaviours and their impact on the situation.

Appropriate open questions at this stage might be:

'How do you think it went?
'What could we do differently?'
'What did we achieve?'

We suggest to our clients that they use a top-tip model called BOOST. It is a model for ensuring that any feedback that a coach gives during a coaching session follows a logical sequence that will make it effective and accepted by the coachee:

Balanced (both things done well and opportunities)
Owned (accepted and recognised by the coachee)
Observed (something that the coach has personally seen)
Specific (concisely explained, demonstrated and relevant)
Timely & trusted (as soon as possible after the observation).

Here are some top tips in relation to giving feedback.

Invite self-assessment:
- create a relationship of openness, honesty and trust;
- probe the coachee to raise awareness;
- listen actively when observing performance and to the coachee's self-assessment;
- summarise without being judgemental; and
- help the coachee to take ownership and responsibility for their actions.

Share observations:
- offer observations and be straightforward;
- be specific;
- focus on behaviour not personality;
- explain potential consequences of behaviour;

- return to self-assessment if necessary to establish shared understanding; and
- ensure that the feedback given can be acted on.

Do make sure as a coach you:
- provide specific examples (what was said or done);
- convey equality in the coaching relationship;
- describe behaviours and do not evaluate; and
- are positive, but balance what was good with areas requiring improvement.

Make sure as a coach you do not:
- generalise or seem vague;
- work with old examples of behaviour;
- use power, for example 'pulling rank';
- act judgementally;
- find fault or blame;
- talk about personality rather than behaviour; or
- use second- or third-hand information.

Step 4: Agree actions

Agreeing actions is a positive step. Be enthusiastic about the opportunities that you, as a coach, have identified with the coachee and let them control and take responsibility for the 'action-taking agenda', with gentle direction from you as the coach.

The step should include clarity on the specific steps required to minimise the gap between the observed performance and the operating standard of the task involved. It is the opportunity to build confidence in the ability of the coachee to improve and achieve the given standard of performance.

It is the coach's responsibility to agree the actions with the coachee and offer continued support.

Follow up after the next call or after they have had a chance to put the actions into practice.

Open questions that may be appropriate during this step include:

> 'What do you think we should do in this case?'
> 'What's the right choice of action?'
> 'What options have we looked at/can we consider?'
> 'What do you think would happen if …?'
> 'Is there any further training that you think would help you to address this opportunity?'

Step 5: Set objectives

The commonly used SMART model provides the ideal template for setting objectives following a coaching session.

SPECIFIC	to the task and clearly defined to achieve the required standard.
MEASURABLE	Described by the standard, action and required levels of achievement.
ACHIEVABLE	Do not set more than two clear improvement areas in an objective.
RELEVANT	Focused on the development need identified for the individual.
TIME BOUND	Time bound, i.e. during the next call or by a certain date.

Open questions that may be appropriate during this step are:

> 'What do we want to achieve?'
> 'What would a good outcome be?'
> 'How stretching are our objectives?'

Remember that objective setting is a key component of a coaching session, so they need to be meaningful, stretching, agreed and above all reviewed at the next coaching session.

The role of questioning and active listening is a key capability for coaches. This screener provides some questions that can be used within each of the five steps of the coaching circle. In coaching sessions these can act as a stimulus when you are coaching, but you must build on them to reflect the needs of the coachee and their applicability for any given situation.

Step	Description
Assess Performance (What performance have you observed?)	Why did that happen? What did we actually observe? Why did we get that reaction? How did you feel when that happened?
Identify the Gap (What performance are we looking for?)	What is happening currently in this account? What do we want to happen? What are we trying to achieve?
Give Feedback (State the situation)	How do you think that went? What did we achieve? What could we do differently?
Agreeing Actions (Gain agreement to change)	What do you think we should do in this case? What's the right choice of actions? What options have we looked at/ can we consider? What would happen if we … ?
Setting Objectives (Describe what's needed?)	What do we want to achieve? How stretching is our objective? What would be an ideal outcome?

Coaching development plan

The coaching development plan should clearly outline the performance of the individual during the period of coaching. It should detail the areas of coaching and the performance level that the individual delivered.

The required performance levels should be in:

- The role profile or job description
- The individual's personal objectives.

There may also be other documents that outline performance levels and requirements; for example, customer plans, project descriptions and others.

The coach should complete the development plan with the person they are coaching and the coachee should agree and sign a copy for their own and the coach's file.

Jobholder	Title:	Manager:
Number of Calls:	Coaching Period:	Duration:
Coaching Needs Agreed: *(List all coaching needs agreed with salesperson)*	Training Action: *(Proposed action to be taken by jobholder / manager to improve job performance e.g. Coaching sessions, courses, further accompaniment*	Responsible for action: By when:
1		
2		
3		
4		
5		
6		
Jobholder's signature:	Manager's signature:	Date:

So in summary, here are the key elements of effective line management coaching.

- Planning and preparation by the coach is essential.
- E D I C – Explanation/Demonstration/Imitation/Consolidation.
- Effective coaching achieves business and personal goals.
- Coaching is an on-the-job process.
- The effective coach appraises performance systematically and objectively.
- Coaching encourages the setting of stretch targets.
- BOOST is an effective way of delivering feedback.
- SMART is an effective way of setting objectives.
- Action planning and follow-up are critical.
- It takes time to coach.

Again, we support the learning by giving participants on a coaching programme the opportunity to complete a self-assessment at the end of the session. This allows them to personally evaluate their learnings from the session.

Self-assessment		
Q1	What is the key message that all coaches should remember?	
	Coaching is really important	
	My line manager is my coach	
	Coaching delivers results	
	Coaching is a worthwhile investment	
Q2	Which of the following is not part of the training cycle?	
	Explanation	
	Demonstration	
	Facilitation	
	Imitation	

Q3	Which behavioural principle is not covered by the coaching model?	
	Patience	
	Consideration	
	Enjoyment	
	Objectivity	
Q4	Which of the following is not a principle of coaching?	
	E D I C	
	Feedback	
	Planning	
	Understanding	
Q5	How many stages does the 'coaching circle' have?	
	Three	
	Four	
	Five	
	Six	
Q6	Objectives should be measured against:	
	The agreed standard for the task	
	Bonus payments	
	The customer's needs	
	The achievement of previous goals	
Q7	The performance gap is:	
	The original objective	
	The achievement during the coaching session	
	The difference between the agreed standard and the performance of the individual	
	The goals that have been agreed with the line manager	

Q8	Which of the following is not recommended when giving feedback?	
	Asking the learner how they think they performed	
	Informing the learner how you think they performed	
	Providing feedback that is balanced, observed and timely	
	Setting the scene in factual terms	
Q9	When agreeing actions with the learner what should you not do?	
	Identify steps to improve performance	
	Stress confidence in the person	
	Suggest ways that they may improve	
	Agree actions and offer support	
Q10	The Coaching Development Plan should not be used to:	
	Set development objectives	
	Record performance levels achieved	
	Encourage self-assessment	
	Build up bonus payments for the learner	
	Total	
	Percentage	

The answers to this self-assessment are:

1)2, 2)3, 3)4, 4)1, 5)3, 6)1, 7)3, 8)2, 9)3, 10)4.

On-the-road coaching

'A critic is a man who knows the way but can't drive the car.'

KENNETH TYNAN, English theatre critic

Many of the tools and techniques identified for effective line management coaching are equally applicable for on-the-road coaching. The programme we recommend for equipping sales management with on-the-road coaching capability are similar to those examined in the previous section.

The major point of differentiation is that it obviously takes place during a salesperson's normal call cycle. In addition to tools like EDIC, BOOST, SMART Objectives and so on, this programme is further supplemented by embedding and practising the use of an on-the-road coaching checklist. This is a powerful tool and part of the documentation process. It's valuable both to the coach and the salesperson. It enables the salesperson to understand the standards that are required, at the same time allowing the coach to follow the structured call or appointment objectively whilst accompanying the salesperson in outlet.

It is a major tool in post call analysis, and encourages and enables the salesperson to review their performance against an identified stage of the call. They are then able to rate themselves against the defined assessment standards.

Following a call the salesperson would rate themselves, and then discuss the rating with their coach. Because of the objectivity of the process there will rarely be any disagreement, the standards being clearly stated and there is little or no ambiguity.

The salesperson will rate themselves as:

1 Exceeding company standard;
2 Meeting company standard;
3 Capable of improvement.

The rating will then be marked on the Route Coaching Checklist for that activity area against the call that they have just made.

The coaching discussion then features around the assessment and its accuracy. Salespeople given an objective rating will often downrate themselves and this the coach needs to address in the same way that an overrating of performance is discussed.

We recommend that the on-the-road coaching checklist is in a small pad format, which enables its use as a working document both in call and after the call. This checklist would be attached to a summary development plan, the same as the one we reviewed within the line management coaching programme. This provides a permanent record for future coaching planning and objective setting.

Each on-the-road coaching checklist is different for each of our clients and indeed types of call. You need to adapt them according to the operational standards expected of the sales team. There is a sample checklist on pages 174–5.

These are the key points to remember about on-the-road coaching.

- Effective on-the-road coaching leads to excellence in execution in retail outlets.
- It ensures that salespeople deliver the required Structured Call or Structured Appointment.

- EDIC – Explanation/Demonstration/Imitation/Consolidation = the way to coach.
- Assessment Standards are the goals of coaching.
- Performance Ratings show how well the salesperson delivers against the standards.
- There are coaching tools available to help both the salesperson and the route coach
- Give feedback on performance as close to the event as possible.
- On-the-road coaching documentation and reporting is for the benefit of the salesperson.

'And when we think we lead, we are most led.'
LORD BYRON, English poet

Having a passion for excellence and inspiring a team are key attributes of effective line managers. They need to understand and occasionally determine the optimum standards of performance required from each and every member of their team. Abdication of the development side of their people does not create a winning team or a respected manager.

Spending time with their people is crucial to coach performance and consequently has to be planned. It is, however, the organisation's responsibility to equip line managers to lead and motivate a group of individuals around common goals.

Having examined how line managers can coach performance on a day-to-day basis, it is vital to give them the skills and confidence to initially train their teams to the required standards.

We have looked at the skills and capabilities necessary to sell exceptional brands, how to package the skills into bite-sized modules and how to coach the capabilities once the salespeople have been trained. This leaves equipping line managers with the confidence and understanding on how to effectively initially train their team.

On the road coaching CHECK LIST		Manager's Name									Salesperson's Name		
NAME OF OUTLET		1	2	3	4	5	6	7	8	9	Overall		
PREPARATION & REPORTING	Personal Organisation												
	Reporting												
	Administration & Equipment												
	Attitude												
SIX STEPS TO SUCCESS 1 PREPARATION	Outlet Calling Objectives												
	Merchandising Materials												
2 APPROACH	Greets Outlet Staff												
	Store Survey												
	Primary Display												
	Secondary Display												
	Competitor Activities												
	Stock Room												
	Other												

3 SALES PRESENTATION	Initial Stock & Order
	Promotion / Other Activity
4 TAKE ACTION	Availability
	Affordability
	Quality
	Visibility
	Persuasion
	Promotion
5 CLOSE THE ORDER	Buying Signals
	Methods of Closing
6 RECORD & EVALUATE	Documents Sales Order
	Sales Record Card
	Competitor Activity
	Follow up Actions
	Learnings for other Calls
	Merchandising Impact
	Personal Performance
SIX SALES TOOLS	PDA
	Sales Presenter
	Sample
	Commercial Proposition
	Pen
	Customer Record

Key learnings	That's interesting

Action plan	
What could I do?	
Who would it involve?	
When should I aim to have it done by?	
What resources or dependencies are involved?	

LOST IN TRANSLATION 8

'You know the phrase, "to take care of something" – well, I realise now that you meant it in a sort of Al Pacino way. Whereas I was thinking more along the lines of Julie Andrews.'

FATHER TED to TOM, Father Ted (Irish sitcom)

Training is the process of bringing a person to a defined and agreed standard of proficiency by practice and instruction. To practise the application of a new skill effectively, learners need the opportunity to contextualise their learning in their day-to-day working environment and have coaching to reach the standard of performance required. We have explored the benefits of line managers taking the responsibility for the development of their teams. We have explored how to turn line managers into coaches and mentors. There is, however, an additional skill required to make line managers great trainers.

There have been numerous occasions when I have had training with boxes ticked to say that I have attended one programme or another, creating an expectation that 'I have been told, so now I know'. In Part I, I shared with you how the brain is connected to building the capability of salespeople. Consequently the packaging and training of operational standards is critical to ensure that learners achieve maximum engagement, retention and recall; it's not boxes ticked on a development plan.

Having examined how to package materials, we now focus on giving line managers the skills to train their teams.

In this chapter we will discover how to train managers to create exceptional learning sessions.

While the content of individual modules defines the 'what', it is imperative for trainers to understand the 'how' and 'why' of training. When we examined how to connect the brain to building capability and the way in which we package skills to equip an organisation, I implied that traditional methods of stand-up training or delivery do not ensure that learners adopt the required standard to the best of their ability. This is certainly my experience.

Understanding how learners learn

The first dynamic for trainers to grasp is the rationale for training to be inclusive. Give learners the opportunity to take responsibility for their training by stepping into the spotlight, as opposed to sitting and listening to a trainer. Unlocking people's commitment allows business change to be inspirational. The same applies to embedding skills and changing behaviour through training.

So the first area of focus for trainers is to understand how learners learn, and thereby connect the construction of training modules to create the historically elusive engagement, retention and recall of learners. To facilitate this you have to show trainers how all the aspects of brain connectivity can be translated into meaningful training sessions, in which learners will thrive through the relevance and enjoyment of the training interaction. To do this you have to engage managers in the learning process, and enable them to apply what they are learning to their personal and professional lives, specifically as trainers of their team, to achieve results. In my business we have a specific module called Mind the Gap.

Our module starts with a number of alternative methods of introductions, or what could be alternatively described as 'settling into the session'. The session construct below reveals an introduction process called W/OW. As we discovered previously, asking learners to introduce themselves is usually only of benefit to the trainer. This method encourages individuals to share a little more about themselves in an alternative medium. W/OW stands for Work and Out of Work. By the trainer modelling W/OW through their own pre-completed W/OW poster they are sharing a method and a number of big learnings at the very start of a learning session.

These are hand-drawn visual posters. It is not an art class but a chance to share a couple of things that are important, at a given point of time, to them in both their business and personal lives.

As an example, this is one relevant for me today. The poster has a clear diagonal divide; it has my name on and defines which area relates to 'work' and which side to 'out of work'.

The images are designed to share a little of my current priorities. In work, they are about ensuring that our current clients remain delighted with all aspects of their interaction with our business, with the second drawing representing this book. Out of work, the two areas identified are firstly my passion for cricket; and secondly, wondering when I am going to find the time to clear up the mounting piles of leaves in our garden. By sharing this, not only will learners understand my priorities in work and a couple of personal areas that are relevant to me, but they would have heard me speak and know my name.

So here is our session construct for Mind the Gap.

- Spotlight from you onto the learners.
- Introductions – model start of W/OW poster – asking learners to pick up a sticky note and a pen and to write what W/OW could mean to them, posting their thoughts onto a W/OW template at the front of the room – model one step at a time.
- Review and reveal what W/OW means in our world.
- Reveal personal pre-completed W/OW poster and share what you have captured on your poster. If it is a large group you may only decide to pick up one point from W and one from OW to speed up the process.
- Suggest to audience that it would be great if we all now completed our own personal W/OW posters – briefing the exercise one step at a time. Take a piece of flip chart paper and a pen and give them 4 minutes 45 seconds to complete their poster. At end of time ask if anyone could benefit from a further 30 seconds.
- Ask if anyone would like to share their poster with the rest of the group first.
- Once each person has introduced their poster, ensure you get a co-facilitator to post them all around the room, leaving them up for the entire workshop.
- Pair and share – ask the learners to talk with the person next to them to establish the benefit of the W/OW posters – take feedback from the group and close the learning loop. For example, look at the similarities with your poster and the ones they have completed – perhaps, how drawings have been used and not words. How they have drawn the divide in the same way as you, how they have learnt something new about a colleague, and so on. Key learning is that learners model/copy what you as a trainer say and do.

Having completed this initial session, it is important to turn attention to understanding why training materials are constructed as they are. For examples, why posters are important, why to use breakout exercises, why there are differing formats of the materials. To facilitate the sharing of this knowledge with the trainers, we run a session off a number of posters placed around the room. The construct of this element of the trainer session is as follows.

- Now that we have completed some introductions, ask who would like to discover a little more about learning styles and environments.
- Ask the group to take note of the posters on the wall and stand under one that they may already know something about or would be keen to find out more about. I will show you what the posters are later in the chapter.
- Ask them to take a sticky note and a pen from under the poster and write on them what the poster means to them. Ask them to share their observations in their sub-groups. Allow them 5 minutes and thirty seconds to record their thoughts.
- Check for more time, and once all of the groups have completed their observations on sticky notes, ask them to go round each poster in turn to review the poster and add any further thoughts that they may have.
- Once back at their original poster, ask them to review all of the comments, consolidate all of the feedback and prepare to summarise their observations to the whole of the group.
- In turn review all of the posters adding any comments, which could either re-emphasise a point already made or add a dimension that may not have been spotted.

The nine pillars of understanding to create successful learning sessions

This session captures the key components we reviewed in Chapter 2. However, here we will examine how to share this knowledge with a group of trainers in an interactive fashion, creating an understanding of how to apply this knowledge when training their teams.

The posters do not have to follow any prescribed order. The illustrations that follow show you the posters. They are visual with very few words. They are not telling people an answer; instead they are open for individual interpretation. For each of these nine illustrations take a moment to look at the drawing and think what it means to you. The text below each one shares what we believe they mean; however, every time we run one of these sessions there are alternative points of learning. The key for a trainer in this session is to ensure that they summarise the key points of learning. So there are no right or wrong answers.

Traditionally, everyone looks at the trainer and thinks: 'Go on then, impress me' or 'Here we go again, another training course'. The role of you as a trainer is to encourage learners to step into the spotlight. At the end of the programme the trainer traditionally leaves, though the content has to stay. *Put the spotlight on the learner*, for they are the most important element of any training activity. Think about and then satisfy their needs through the content and methodology used. Their comfort with the subject, what they know and what they don't know are important. Enable them to contribute in the best way possible.

There is a distinction between training and learning. Training is something that is done to someone, while learning is something that individuals do for themselves. Ask the learners to consider what is in it for them, their team and the organisation.

We all learn at a different pace – we have to allow learners to absorb the content in different ways and at different speeds. This means that you require a variety of materials and learners should be able to access the points of learning beyond the classroom. This can be through reviewing their participant manuals, personal learning logs, e-learning sites and other means. If you, as a trainer, do not *create a love for learning*, people will not learn. The personal enthusiasm of a trainer is infectious and therefore essential.

It is the learning that is important, not the instruction. Briefing tasks *one step at a time* ensures that learners can follow the learning process as opposed to worrying about whether they are doing the right thing at the right time.

Examples of this could be:

- 'Find a partner that you have not worked with yet today.'
- 'Take a sticky note.'
- 'Pick up a pen.'
- 'Write down your ideas.'
- 'Prepare to share your ideas with others.'
- 'Place your sticky note on the flip chart next to me.'

Research has identified that as much as *99% of all learning is sub-conscious*. We all learn through experiences. A surprisingly small amount comes from what we are told. Create the environment where the learners can touch, feel and explore the materials, and work out for themselves the difference it will make to them and the organisation. Learning will always be a mixture of experiences, and it is your responsibility to tap into the subconscious through all the methods available to you. These can include learning activities/role-plays, experiential learning, visual messages, intrapersonal and interpersonal activities and in many more ways.

Posters are an easy way to reinforce key messages. Learners find them intriguing. If you use a computer-generated slide presentation in learning environments the message is on the screen one moment and then gone the next. You can refer to posters time and again. Learners will readily be able to recall the image that they saw. *Posters are permanent.*

Here are a couple of tips about using posters.

- Use a border; it focuses learners into the message.
- Don't put them up straight – tilting the head to read a poster or message means that the body's blood flow changes = more oxygen to the brain = more receptive to learning.

After 25 minutes sitting down we all take in 15% less information, due to poor supply of oxygenated blood to the brain. Simply by *changing the 'state'* of the learners, their ability and appetite to learn is significantly enhanced. Examples of state changes include:

- moving around/standing up;
- moving to a different part of the room;
- working on their own or in groups;
- working in pairs;
- having a brainstorming session;
- asking learners to reflect on a point and capture their observations in their learning log book;
- having a five minute break ... and so on.

As a trainer you have to use inclusive language, and then demonstrate behaviour to maximise engagement from learners. Using language like 'I want you to …', 'find a partner' and similar just creates a divide between you and the learners and is to no one's benefit. Far better would be the use of inclusive language like 'It would help us if we now …', and 'let's get into pairs.'

By demonstrating the desired behaviour you ensure that learners understand what is expected from them. Whether it is picking up a specific piece of material when you want them to, or writing a comment in your own log book will ensure that learners are engaged in understanding specific tasks and modelling what you say and do. If you as a trainer do something, the more chance that the learners will do the same. *Learners model what you say and do.*

Although *everyone enters learning sessions with different levels of skills and experiences*, the end result of a training session should be the creation of a common way – regardless of past experience.

It is vital that you label the learning experience – 'At the end of today we will have ...'. Always anchor a session or topic. This means effectively summarising/discussing what has been learnt. For example, running a breakout exercise should always follow the same format.

- Brief delegates on the exercise.
- Run the exercise.
- Summarise the key points using a poster, or by asking the learners to reflect on their personal or group learnings from the exercise.

Here is where we showcase the thinking of Professor Gardner – that *everyone learns in different ways*. It is important to ensure that materials are constructed so that we appeal to as many of the learning intelligences as possible. See Chapter 2 to refresh yourself on the eight intelligences that Gardner identified.

Establishing the confidence to train

'Do not worry about not being able to master a skill; what one has to be concerned about is lack of perseverance. One's skill cannot be perfected without perseverance in practice.'

Chinese proverb

Once line managers have grasped, occasionally with great clarity, the benefits of training in the manner we have just examined, their appetite quickly turns to a wish to start training their teams and reaping what they perceive to be clear benefits. There is, however, a clear difference between knowing it and doing it. We therefore ensure that through the train-the-trainer environment, line managers have the opportunity both to familiarise themselves with the materials and to practise delivering a selection of modules to each other in what is a safe environment. The learnings here are often similar.

- It is not as easy as it looks.
- It takes time to prepare to run a session.
- Knowing how to do something is not the same as teaching someone to do it.

Over the course of a one- or one-and-a-half-day programme, line managers have the opportunity to review all the components of a training module. They break up modules into smaller chunks and practise delivering them to each other. They work out what they need to do in order to personalise the material for their team. This can include adding specific anecdotes into their trainer notes, building in content that reaffirms their team's local priorities and so forth. The 'safe' environment of a train-the-trainer forum allows them to practise, learn from mistakes, and receive coaching from their peers and trainers. Ultimately they learn what they need to do in order to prepare for any future training interaction with their team.

Once their confidence has been established, they can follow a similar level of preparation for any future modules that are cascaded to them when they are relevant to any future priorities of the organisation.

Key learnings	That's interesting

Action plan	
What could I do?	
Who would it involve?	
When should I aim to have it done by?	
What resources or dependencies are involved?	

PUTTING IT ALL TOGETHER **9**

'One does not discover new lands without consenting to leave sight of the shore.'

ANDRÉ GIDE, *French author and Nobel prize winner for literature 1947*

Quotations, for me, create relevance and meaning while sparking inspiration. This maxim, written by André Gide, has inspired me for many years. Defining your vision, working out exactly how to attain it and having the conviction to thread your way towards a new way of working or opportunity in life is critical to attaining your goals.

When I was a child, on many occasions I crossed the English Channel by ferry to visit family in Europe. This stretch of sea is only about thirty miles wide. There comes a time in the journey when you can look back and see the white cliffs of Dover, and then you turn the other way and see the French coast. A couple of minutes later you glance back at England and all you can see is the horizon. At that point, when I was five or six years old, I felt I was away from home and that is when home sickness kicked in. At the same time I was looking forward to what lay ahead. The moral of this is that wherever your destination lies, there will be a time when you have to leave your known world behind.

Much the same applies to the world of creating an organisation that is customer- as well as consumer-centric – an organisation where sales teams are turned into profit heroes through defined operational standards, skills and capabilities that are trained and coached by passionate line managers, and where customers recognise your business as their supplier of choice – because of your outstanding brands, propositions and people. This is a prize worth taking leave of the familiar.

Having journeyed through the framework for 'Turning your sales force into profit heroes', in this chapter we will:

- ensure we never lose sight of the needs of the learners;
- establish where to start the journey and the steps to achieve the goal; and
- learn how to listen, learn and satisfy the needs of your customers.

Spotlight on the learners: first and always

Embracing new ways of working is a journey and not a destination. There will always be the necessity for a business to evolve. The changing needs of customers and consumers, your innovation agenda, the growth of your competitors, new channels and other challenges will always require a measured and dextrous approach to managing the sales function.

We have seen how we are individually shaped by the behaviour of those around us, how it makes sense to connect the brain to building capability, the benefits that the clarity of role and skills of each individual within the team can bring. The key to embedding change is not only enrolling every person within the organisation, but also thinking through and defining a plan that will take the organisation on the journey. Remember, no matter how far one is looking to travel, every journey starts with a single step.

Paul Walsh, the CEO of Diageo plc, wrote in the foreword that he is passionately sponsoring the role of his sales function. Sponsorship is not a choice – it is an imperative. Individuals within any business are focused on achieving their objectives – you get what you measure. Ensuring there is enthused passion and commitment to the sales agenda, all the way from the helm of the business to the salesperson nurturing amazing relationships with customers drives change, but this change will only happen with sponsorship from every member of the leadership population.

This journey is not one of revolution but one of evolution. It occasionally takes courage to embark on change, but courage is repaid by the realisation that the benefits for individuals, teams and the organisation is a prize that everyone will embrace.

Members of the sales team always have an eye on their current priorities, undoubtedly including their targets today, next week, next month and next quarter. The role of their line managers has to be to support them in delivering this business-critical performance, while at the same time releasing the latent talent of each member of their team through measured, high-quality training and coaching. Taking one step at a time will mean that skills and capabilities can be developed in tandem to achieve the agreed business agenda.

There will come a time when learners realise that there is a focus on their personal development, that their line managers are amazing coaches and that their relationships with customers are going from strength to strength. They will realise that this is an environment for them where they can fulfil their aspirations, enjoy their relationships with peers, colleagues and customers, and be supported by an organisation that focuses as much on the needs of its customers as on the needs of the consumers.

As we reflected in Chapter 2, giving a briefing on exercises to a group of learners one step at a time is a way of guiding individuals effectively through a learning experience, without confusing them with complicated instructions. Much the same applies to skills and capability development. My focus has been on the definition of the role of the salesperson, developing high quality modules to build a common level of core skill, and equipping line managers to be outstanding trainers and coaches.

As the model in Chapter 6 defined, core skills of selling alone will not maximise opportunities with customers. There are many additional attributes of highly effective salespeople, of which negotiating capability and joint working with customers are but two. When constructing a building much of the investment is below the ground, but is essential to a functional structure. Much the same applies to selling skills; getting the core skills embedded into habits will lay the foundations of a great sales team. This has to be done one step at a time, with eyes firmly fixed on delivering today while maximising tomorrow.

Defining where maximum opportunity lies, and then prioritising the aspects of skill and capability development, are essential. Individuals will not be able to adopt new ways of working if they are being asked to embrace too many new things all at once.

Where to start

> *'Let's start at the very beginning. It's a very good place to start.'*
>
> **RODGERS and HAMMERSTEIN,**
> *The Sound of Music ('Do-Re-Mi')*

Embedding behavioural or procedural change within organisations stems from a combination of establishing the benefit, introducing effective learning processes and blending them with hard pragmatic measures. The question to ask is 'What happens before and after the training intervention that tells the learner that the business *means* this; and that the application of the learnt skills is mandatory?'

Proactive endorsement and vocal sponsorship is essential. If focus is purely centred on the adaptation of the sales team's skills and capability with an absence of understanding of 'what's in it for me', and 'what's in it for the organisation', the prescribed changes in ways of working will not be adopted. The salesperson must be able to recognise the alignment between the messages contained within a learning event and what they believe to be the corporate strategic objectives. The single biggest measure here is ensuring that learners are not abandoned, but feel empowered through on-going sponsorship of any advocated changes to ways of working.

Organisations have to make certain that the way that learning happens ensures that not only is it aligned to the strategic objectives of the organisation, but more critically, that all learners are motivated in the journey as they move effectively and quickly from learner to doer.

That then points us to where to start. It's about understanding where you are, where you want to be and defining the gap. Combine that with proactive and engaging sponsorship.

This model represents how we believe an organisation needs to flow through establishing the size of the potential prize to measuring and evaluating the ongoing benefit.

Each organisation differs from others in some way, and therefore the solutions will always be different.

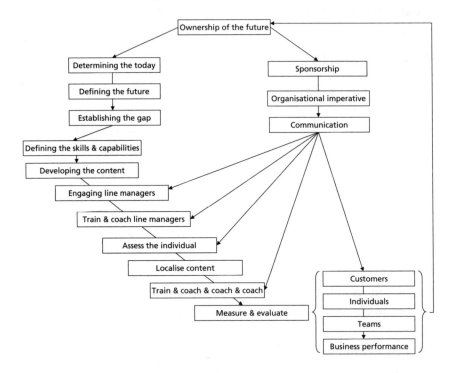

Listening to and learning from your customers

I passionately believe that the world does not need any more consultants who go into organisations and tell them what, in their opinion, they should be doing about any issue or opportunity. Organisations differentiate themselves not only by their products and marketing expertise, but also by clearly defining what their customers want and creating bespoke solutions.

Coupled with detailed organisational assessments, over the last few years we have developed a business tool that helps to 'Unlock your Strength at Retail' through the voice of your customer. Through a short, high impact and highly adaptable web-based questionnaire we canvas and collate the views of customers and distributors as well as internal employees. Hearing the views of customers provides organisations with a deeper customer understanding, and ultimately identifies opportunities for any customer-centric change. This in turn initiates and drives competitive advantage to take a business forward.

The power of hearing verbatim comments from customers will generate immediate change. The numerical data will provide measurement and 'key performance indicators'. Bringing the voice of the customer and other key stakeholders right into the heart of your organisation, identifying the current leadership position and highlighting both performance and perception gaps determines opportunity. The insights and recommendations derived from the data underpin sales strategy; they create sustainable customer relationships, frontline operating standards and sales force development.

We recommend seeking feedback on an informal basis through high quality, top-to-top relationships with key customers that are then supplemented through a formal annual feedback process. This informs the sales strategy and measures the impact of any customer-centric change journey. Typically we would recommend seeking feedback from customers in six principal areas.

- **Leadership**
  Do you lead in the market?
- **Expertise**
  Do you have the right expertise to win?
- **Performance**
  Are you delivering growth for everyone?
- **Efficiency**
  Are you leveraging your strength at retail?
- **Partnership**
  Does everyone work together for mutual and consumer benefit?
- **Values barometer**
  Do you share perspectives of performance against the organisational values?

The single biggest determinant around driving a step change in organisations customer-centric capability is *people*: after all, as we established, that is why 75% of what you plan to change will not happen. Knowing where to go and what to do takes you some of the way. This, coupled with an enthused team who are working together to delight customers, and in turn consumers, with pride and passion for the organisation and the products they sell does lead to a world of transformational performance.

Key learnings	That's interesting

Action plan	
What could I do?	
Who would it involve?	
When should I aim to have it done by?	
What resources or dependencies are involved?	

NOT SURE/WANT TO LEARN MORE

10

'The early bird may catch the worm, but it's the second mouse that gets the cheese.'

JON HAMMOND, US musician

While reading and dipping in and out of this book, many thoughts will have occurred to you. You may have used some, or even all of the areas to capture your personal learnings and action plans at the end of each chapter. Perhaps you have made notes, spoken to colleagues, or used the self-assessment section on operating standards. One thing is for certain; and that is, I am sure you will have identified any number of things that you could do to improve your sales teams.

I encourage learners to personalise their learning in a training session and give them options to extend their participation afterwards; I find the same applies to me when I read a book. I am either awaiting the publication of the next episode in a series or trying to find out more about loops of interest that the author has created – particularly when it is a business or factual publication. This chapter is designed to point you to a few different areas where you may wish to extend your learning and how to prioritise the action areas you have identified.

Consolidating your learnings

There are nine chapters contained within this book which have a template at the end for you to capture your key learnings, observations and action plans.

Using the template on the next page to consolidate and prioritise your actions relative to each other, will assist you in hypothesising the ease of implementation and size of prize for your organisation.

Chapter	Action number	Size of prize 10 = high 1 = low	Ease of implementation 10 = easy 1 = hard
Are you responsible for the way others behave?	1a		
	1b		
	1c		
Connecting the brain to building capability	2a		
	2b		
	2c		
What's in it for the organisation?	3a		
	3b		
	3c		
The capabilities necessary to sell exceptional brands	4a		
	4b		
	4c		
The skills to sell exceptional brands	5a		
	5b		
	5c		
Packaging the skills to equip the organisation	6a		
	6b		
	6c		
Inspirational sales leadership	7a		
	7b		
	7c		
Lost in translation	8a		
	8b		
	8c		
Putting it all together	9a		
	9b		
	9c		

Having consolidated your actions, now use the prioritisation matrix opposite to determine the relativity of your actions in terms of size of prize and ease of implementation. This identifies the areas where you will be able to unlock immediate benefit, and consequently inform the logical sequence to turning your sales force into profit heroes.

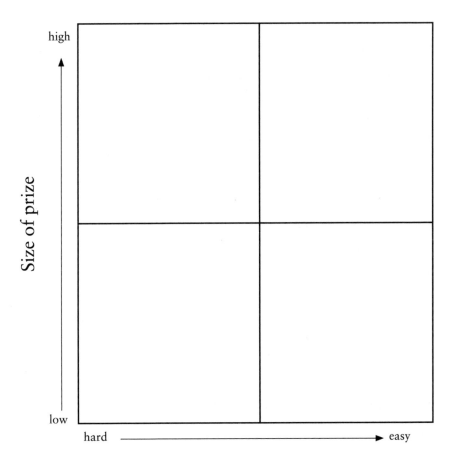

Publications

I have cited a number of writers who have inspired me in studying how people learn, and the skills of highly effective individuals. I could create a huge list, but for me three is a good starting number, so I would like to recommend to you:

- Howard Gardner: *Frames of Mind.*
- Tim Andrews: *Where's your Spotlight?*
- Stephen Covey: *Seven Habits of Highly Effective People.*

Illustrations

There are a number of models and templates in this book, but I find exceptional meaning comes through the illustration of key messages. I trawled extensively to find an illustrator who could add to my written word and found Steve Chadburn. If you would like to contact him and have his style support you, I couldn't recommend him highly enough. You can contact Steve at: www.steve-chadburn.com

Fancy a go yourself?

I mentioned that writing this book is probably one of the biggest journeys I have ever undertaken. Having the support of an outstanding publisher is not only important, but critical. The whole team at Infinite Ideas have been challenging and supportive at the same time – a rare combination. If you would like to find out more about authoring a book yourself, you should pay a visit to: www.infideas.com

Accessing a component of my inspiration

There are many experiences that influence how we are. In the world of business I have made reference to one of my big inspirations being the time that I spent working for Guinness and Diageo plc. If you would like to read some more about the world's leading premium drinks company, visit: www.diageo.com

Personalising your learning

The most powerful bank of knowledge that you have is made from your own thoughts, notes and ideas. I would encourage you to spend time determining what opportunities may be awaiting you and your business. Canvas the opinions and enrol the support of others for the vision that you have, and start to invigorate your peers and colleagues behind the opportunities and success that can be attained by 'Turning your sales force into profit heroes'.

Contacting REL Field Marketing

This sister company to REL Sales Consulting specialises in field marketing, principally within the United Kingdom. We manage outsourced field sales teams. In 2008 one of our teams was recognised as the best field sales team in the UK.

We work strategically with clients in all areas of in-store activation, including merchandising, compliance, audit, sampling, mystery shopping and experiential marketing campaigns. There is a dedicated tactical division, managing around 30,000 retail visits per year. If you would like to know more about the range of services that REL offers to its field marketing clients, and how we could support your business, please visit: www.relfm.com

Accessing REL Sales Consulting

'Unlocking your strength at retail' is the phrase that we use to epitomise the support that we provide to our clients. As well as sales capability and customer insight generation, this extends to subjects such as optimisation of trade pricing and terms, route to market assessments, talent development strategies and solutions, senior level one-to-one coaching, speaking to sales-based audiences and other related areas. If you would like to get in contact with REL Sales Consulting you can e-mail: info@relsc.com or visit our website: www.relsc.com

INDEX

alternative close, 120
assessment *see* performance assessment
assumptive close, 120

behavioural principles
    coaching, 16–21, 159, 164
    operational standards, 85–6
    role model, 12–15
BOOST model, 163
building capability
    framework, 126–30
    learning extensions, 147–8
    learning logbook, 141
    packaging modules, 131–4, 148–9
    participant manual, 138–40
    programme objectives and session
      construct, 132–4
    self-assessment screeners, 144–7
    supporting tools and materials,
      143–4
    trainer manual, 135–6, 135–8
    training time, 130
    see also coaching capabilities; core
      skills; effective practice; learning
      processes

call and selling tools, 61–3
capabilities *see* building capability;
    coaching capabilities

Chadburn, Steve, 208
channel strategy, 67–9
closing the deal, 117–22, 132–3
coaching capabilities
    behavioural principles, 16–21, 159,
      164
    BOOST model, 163
    coaching circle (EDIC model),
      158–9
      agree actions, 164–5
      assess performance, 161
      feedback, 162–4
      identify the gap, 162
      set objectives, 165–6
    development plans, 166–70
    embedding, 5–7, 28–30, 197–8
    facilitating/sponsoring, 154–7
    feedback, 159, 162–4
    module steps, 156
    on-the-road, 171–3
    planning interventions, 160
    self assessment screeners, 168–70
    see also building capability; learning
      processes
coaching circle *see* EDIC model
company strategy
    embedded solutions, xi–xiii, 6–7,
      27–9, 197–8
    flow chart model, 198

globalisation, 3–4, 52–3
    outlet segmentation, 58–63
    performance measurement, 15
    sales organisation, 2–4, 50–3
        evolution and innovation, 194–7
        proactive sponsorship, 198–9
    see also operational standards
consultative selling, 113–18
conversational structure, 101–4
core skills, 90–3
    closing the deal, 117–22
        screener example, 132–3
    consultative selling, 113–17
    foundation skills, 93–4
        conversational structure, 101–4
        features and benefits, 107–9
        listening and questioning, 94–6
        overcoming objections, 104–7
        recognising different personal
            styles, 97–101
    structured call and selling tools,
        61–3
    see also building capability; sales
        force
customer orientation
    awareness of competition, 5, 90–4
    customer business planning, 69–72
    customer needs, 110–12
    customer priorities, 107–9
    customer relationships, 73–7, 84
    listening and questioning, 94–6
        feedback, 198–200

demographics, 2–3
Diageo plc, 208
    see also Walsh, Paul

EDIC model (coaching circle), 158–9
    agree actions, 164–5
    assess performance, 161
    feedback, 162–4
    identify the gap, 162
    set objectives, 165–6
embedded solutions, 5–7, 28–30, 197–8

employees *see* core skills; operational
    standards; sales force
exceptional brands, 90–122

features and benefits, 107–9
feedback
    BOOST model, 163
    coaching, 159, 162–3
    customer questionnaires, 198–200
foundation skills, 93–4
    conversational structure, 101–2
    features and benefits, 107–9
    listening and questioning, 94–6
    overcoming objections, 104–7
    recognising different personal styles,
        97–101

Gardner, Howard, *Frames of Mind*, 26,
    190
globalisation, 3–4, 52–3
good practice standards *see* operational
    standards

key account teams, 58–61
    structured call and selling tools,
        61–3
    see also operational standards

leadership *see* building capability
learning processes
    consolidation and implementation,
        205–7
    differing talents and skills, 24–7, 37,
        189–90
    embedding solutions, 6–7, 27–9,
        197–8
    environment, 33–4, 38–9, 187
    experience, 36, 185–6
    language, 35, 188
    publications on, 207
    relevance and response, 27, 29–33,
        183–4, 189
        clarity, 32–3
    understanding, 179–82

visual support tools, 39–40, 208
  posters, 179–81, 186
  see also building capability; coaching
    capabilities
line management *see* building capability;
    coaching capabilities; core skills
listening and learning, 94–6, 198–200
  coaching, 166

Master Trainer framework, 29
McGuire, Patrick, 47
Meyer, Herbert, 3
Mind the Gap module, 179–82

operational standards, 58
  area of best practice, 81–2
  assessment, 82–4
  behavioural impact, 85–6
  channel strategy, 67–9
  customer business planning, 69–72
  identifying, 63–5
  managing customer relationships,
    73–7
    skills and capability, 84
  measurement of performance, 80–1
  point of purchase (POP) execution,
    77–9
  sales strategy, 85
  see also company strategy; key
    account teams; sales force
organisation structures, 2–4, 50–3
outlet segmentation, 58–63
overcoming objections, 104–7
  selling a proposition, 107–9

performance assessment, 15
  coaching circle format, 161–6
    and development plan, 166–70
  on-the-road coaching, 171–5
  self-assessment screeners, 144–7,
    168–70
  selling exceptional brands, 80–4
point of purchase (POP) execution,
    77–9

propositions, 107–9
publications, 207, 208

recognition of different personal styles,
    97–101
REL Sales Consulting, 209

sales force
  commitment and recognition, 44–8
    effective practice, 48–50
  company strategy and, xi–xiii, 2–4,
    50–4, 194–9
  key account teams, 58–61
    structured call and selling tools,
    61–3
  team operating structures, 50–1
  see also building capability; core
    skills; operational standards
self-assessment screeners, 144–7,
    168–70
SMART model, 165
special benefits close, 120
sponsorship, 195, 197–8
  facilitating coaching capabilities,
    154–7
  see also Walsh, Paul
standards of practice *see* operational
    standards
styles, recognising different personal,
    97–101
summary close, 119

team operating structures, 50–1
training *see* building capability;
    coaching capabilities; learning
    processes

visual support tools, 39–40, 208
  posters, 179–81, 186

W/OW process, 179–81
Walsh, Paul, 'The Diageo Way of
    Selling,', xi–xiii, 27
  see also Diageo plc; sponsorship